1858	East India Company's rule replaced by that of a viceroy appointed by the British crown
1862	Archaeological Survey established
1877	Queen Victoria proclaimed Empress of India
1877-1947	Anand V. Coomaraswamy, renowned Indologist and art historian of the 20th century. Born in Sri Lanka
1885	Indian National Congress inaugurated in Bombay
1893	Mohandas K. Gandhi (1869-1948) begins 20-year career as a lawyer in South Africa
1906	Muslim League founded
1911	World's first official airmail flight from Allahabad to Naini
1913	Rabindranath Tagore, artist, writer, musician, and philosopher, awarded Nobel Prize for literature
1916	Moderate, extremist, and Muslim League leaders agree on demand for a national legislative assembly to be elected on a communal basis
1919	Montagu-Chelmsford Reforms provide for legislative assembly to begin in 1921 Amritsar massacre
1930	Civil Disobedience Movement launched. Gandhi undertakes salt march
	Muhammad Iqbal (1873-1938) proposes separate state for India's Muslims
1934	Indian women first made eligible to vote in elections for the central legislature
1940	Muslim League, under President Mhd. Ali Jinnah demands creation of a sovereign Muslim state
1941	Jawaharlal Nehru writes *Toward Freedom* (autobiography)
1945-1947	British Labor Government prepares to grant India complete self-government
1946	Jawaharlal Nehru writes *The Discovery of India* (history)
1947	India, under Prime Minister Jawaharlal Nehru, and Pakistan, under Prime Minister Liaquat Ali Khan become independent dominions
1947	University of Pennsylvania establishes first South Asia regional studies program in the United States
1948	Mohandas Gandhi assassinated in New Delhi
	Death of Mhd. Ali Jinnah (born 1876)
1950	B.R. Ambedkar drafts Indian Constitution; secular state is established and untouchability is abolished
1950-1960	Tours by Ravi Shankar and Ali Akbar Khan lead to worldwide popularization of Indian music
1951	First volume of *The History and Culture of the Indian People*, edited by R. Majumdar, is published
1952	First general elections held in India
1953	Crafts Museum set up in New Delhi
1954	National Gallery of Modern Art established in New Delhi
1956	First atomic reactor in South Asia begins operation in Trombay, India
1959	Door Darshan (TV). First TV program in Delhi is broadcast
1961	First International Congress of Asian Archaeology held in New Delhi
1961	National Institute of Design set up in Ahmedabad
1963	First rocket launching facility set up in India
1964	Lal Bahadur Shastri elected Prime Minister upon the death of Jawaharlal Nehru
1966	Indira Gandhi elected Prime Minister
1971	Establishment of the Department of Culture
1977	Morarji Desai elected Prime Minister
1978-1979	*Aditi* exhibition first held in New Delhi
1980	Indira Gandhi elected to her final term as Prime Minister
1982	*Aditi* exhibition held at the Barbican Centre, London
	Prime Minister Indira Gandhi and President Ronald Reagan agree on a cultural exchange in 1985-86, resulting in the Festival of India Year and the Aditi Exhibition at the Smithsonian
1983	India hosts the Summit of Non-Aligned Nations in New Delhi
1984	First Indian astronaut speaks to Indian TV from orbit
October, 1984	Prime Minister Indira Gandhi assassinated in New Delhi
December, 1984	Rajiv Gandhi elected Prime Minister

This chronology was compiled in part from the following sources:

The Rise of Civilization in India and Pakistan. F.R. Allchin and Bridget Allchin, 1982. Cambridge University Press.

Sources of Indian Tradition, volumes I and II. Edited by W.T. DeBary, 1958. New York: Columbia University Press.

A Historical Atlas of South Asia. Edited by Joseph E. Schwartzberg, 1978. University of Chicago Press.

Aditi
The Living Arts of India

FESTIVAL
OF INDIA
1985-1986

Published on the occasion of
the exhibition, *Aditi—A Celebration of Life*,
organized for the Festival of India 1985-1986
at the Thomas M. Evans Gallery of
the National Museum of Natural History,
Smithsonian Institution, Washington, D.C.
June 4-July 28, 1985

Smithsonian Institution Press
Washington, D.C.

p. 1: This terra cotta mother goddess and child dates to the Kushan period, 1-100 A.D. The exact provenance of this figure, which is of a child held close to its mother's breast, is not known. However, in recent excavations at Sringaverpur, near Allahabad in Uttar Pradesh state, similar mother goddesses were found and appear to have been votive offerings to the water deity for the protection of children.

Mother Goddess and Child. *1-100 A.D. Terra cotta, 10 x 5½″ (26 x 14½ cm). Collection of Pupul Jayakar, New Delhi.*

p. 2: Out of Hindu mythology comes the legend of *Kāma Dhenu* (the fulfiller of wishes), who emerged from the ocean of milk that was churned by the gods and the demons. The cow with full udders is an auspicious symbol of prosperity.

Kāma Dhenu. *18th century. Painted wooden manuscript cover, 12⅛ x 5⅝″ (33 x 13 cm). Asutosh Museum of Indian Art, Calcutta.*

Right: Graceful movement and colorful dress characterize the ancient daily ritual of fetching water from the village well.

Festival of India 1985-1986

Patrons: The Honorable Rajiv Gandhi,
             Prime Minister of India
             Mrs. Ronald Reagan

In India:

   Chairman, Indian Advisory Committee,
   Mrs. Pupul Jayakar

   Director General S.K. Misra

   Coordinator Vijay Singh

The exhibition was organized in India
by The Handicrafts and Handlooms
Export Corporation of India, Ltd.
(HHEC), Diljeet Aurora, Chairman,
with the support of the Office of the
Development Commissioner,
Handicrafts.

In the United States:

   *Chairman, American National
   Committee and Smithsonian
   Secretary Emeritus* S. Dillon
   Ripley

   *Executive Director, Indo-U.S.
   Subcommission on Education and
   Culture,* Ted M. G. Tanen

   *Assistant Director, Indo-U.S.
   Subcommission on Education and
   Culture,* Patrice Fusillo

In India and the United States:

   *Aditi Project Director
   Exhibition Curator and
   Designer* Rajeev Sethi

   Aditi Project Consultant M.N.
   Deshpande

   *Festival of India Coordinator and
   Minister (Culture), Embassy of
   India,* Niranjan Desai

Manufactured in the United States of
America
Aditi The Living Arts of India
Library of Congress Catalog Card Number:
85-50439
ISBN 0-87474-852-6
    0-87474-853-3 (paperback ed.)

Pages 254–266: "Kantha Textiles," "The
Image of the Horse," *and a portion of* "The
Role of the Professional Craftsman" *first
appeared in* Unknown India: Ritual Art in
Tribe and Village *by Stella Kramrisch (1968),
and was reprinted with permission of The Philadelphia Museum of Art, and later appeared in*
Exploring India's Sacred Art: Selected Writings of Stella Kramrisch. *Philadelphia: University of Pennsylvania Press, 1983.*

Smithsonian Institution

   Secretary Robert McC. Adams

   Assistant Secretary for Public Service
   Ralph Rinzler

   *Program Manager, Smithsonian
   Festival of India Programs*
   Jeffrey LaRiche

   Smithsonian Institution Press

      Director Felix C. Lowe

      Managing Editor Maureen Jacoby

      Editor Patricia Gallagher

      Editorial Assistant Jeanne Sexton

      Picture Editor Frances C. Rowsell

      Production Manager Lawrence J. Long

      Production Assistant Kathleen Brown

      *Art Director, Office of Folklife
      Programs and* Aditi
      Catalogue Designer Daphne
      Shuttleworth

   Office of Folklife Programs

      Director Peter Seitel

      Aditi Program Coordinator Richard
      Kurin

      Aditi Assistant Program Coordinator
      Jonathan Mark Kenoyer

      Aditi Cultural Liaison Nita Kumar

      Program Specialist Arlene Liebenau

   National Museum of Natural History

      Director Richard S. Fiske

      Assistant Director for Exhibitions
      Laurence P. O'Reilly

      Coordinator, Special Exhibits Sheila
      M. Mutchler

      *Assistant Coordinator, Special
      Exhibits* Marjory G. Stoller

      Aditi Project Manager Constance T.
      Lee

      Exhibits Writer/Editor Sue Nell
      Voss

      Education Specialist Laura L.
      McKie

      Public Information Officer Thomas
      R. Harney

      Aditi Project Liaison, New Delhi
      Rochelle Kessler

      Designers for the Aditi Exhibition
      Elizabeth Miles and Richard
      Molinaroli of Miles,
      Friedberg, and Molinaroli, Inc.

Note: The name of the All-India Handicrafts Board Crafts Museum, New Delhi,
referred to in the captions as the AIHB
Crafts Museum, recently has been
changed to the National Handicrafts
and Handlooms Museum.

Opposite: Against a backdrop
of homing cattle in the honey-
colored light of a late Indian
afternoon, an older girl is
minding a baby asleep in the
type of cradle characteristic
of Gujarat.

p.10: Elaborate headdress
worn by folk dancer for the
Thayyam ritual dance per-
formed in north Kerala.

Front cover:
At Shadipur Depot, outside
Delhi, Bhopā balladeer
Ram Karan, his wife Gotli
Devi, and sons Shish Ram
and Kailash, and Harji Lol
perform before a scroll that
depicts the story of the
Rajput warrior, Pābūjī.
Back cover:
Detail of the scroll that
illustrates the story of
Pābūjī.

Guide to Transcription and Pronunciation

The non-English words that appear in this book derive from a variety of major languages, including Sanskrit, Tamil, Arabic, and Persian, and represent a wide range of Indian dialects: Hindi, Urdu, Rajasthani, Marwari, Bengali, Marathi, Gujurati, Kannada, Telegu, Malayalam, etc. Although, for the convenience of the reader, we have chosen not to use the detailed diacritical marks employed in most academic texts, we have retained the use of the super-scripted - to indicate long vowels, with the exception of words that are the officially recognized spellings of Indian states and place names and the personalized transcriptions of names of individuals.

Guide to Pronunciation

a	as *u* in but
ā	as *a* in father
i	as *i* in pin
ī	as *i* in machine
u	as *u* in pull
ū	as *u* in rule
ri (a vowel)	as *er* in river
e	as *ay* in say
ai	as *ai* in aisle
o	as *o* in go
au	as *ow* in how
ch	as *ch* in church
sh	as *sh* in shape
g	as *g* in get
kh	as *kh* in lakehouse
gh	as *gh* in doghouse
th	as *th* in anthill
dh	as *dh* in roundhouse
bh	as *bh* in clubhouse
ph	as *ph* in uphill

Guide to the Pronunciation of Persian and Indo-Persian Words

Short Vowels

a	Intermediate between the vowels in the English words *bed* and *bad*
i	As the vowel sound in the English *fen*
u	As in the English word *put*

Long Vowels

ā	as *a* in father
ī	as *i* in police
u	as *u* in prude

Diphthongs

ai	as *ey* in they
au	as *ou* in out

Adapted from
Sources of Indian Tradition.
William Theodore de Bary, ed.
New York: Columbia University Press, 1958

7

To Mrs. Indira Gandhi, 1917-1984

It seems especially fitting that the Sanskrit word *aditi*, denoting "creative power," has been chosen to signify the participation of nearly 20 Smithsonian bureaus in the Festival of India, a series of cultural events being organized by institutions across the United States in 1985 and 1986. Throughout its history, the Smithsonian has been creatively involved with India. Such involvement is reflected in the collections of our museums which contain a range of artifacts from Hindu and Buddhist sculptures of the third century B.C. to the meteoric dagger of the seventeenth-century Mughal emperor, Jahangir, and the nation's largest collection of Indian stamps and coins. It is also seen in myriad scholarly research projects sponsored by the Smithsonian, such as the ornithological research of my distinguished predecessor, S. Dillon Ripley. We are delighted, thus, to have the opportunity of joining this unprecedented nationwide celebration of a vibrant and complex civilization which faces, as do we all, immense challenges.

That India is a land of contrasts is well known. It is the world's largest democracy and second most populous nation. It is a land that is becoming rapidly industrialized and technologically advanced while remaining a cradle for many ancient cultures which have maintained their traditions to this day.

This book explores one area of India's vast and fabled heritage: the impact of performance, crafts, and myth on the world of the child as he traverses the cycle of life in traditional Indian society. It has been published to accompany the brilliant exhibition, *Aditi—A Celebration of Life*, which was first mounted in New Delhi for the International Year of the Child and again in 1982 as part of the London Festival of India. This unique exhibition, with its 2000 objects and 40 artisans and performers, has been brought to the Smithsonian as part of our observance of the year of India.

The idea for the Festival of India as a comprehensive presentation of culture originated with India's late prime minister, Mrs. Indira Gandhi. It is particularly appropriate that we dedicate this volume to her memory: her vision for India and devotion to the arts continue to inspire us all in furthering international understanding through cultural exchange.

Robert McC. Adams
Secretary
Smithsonian Institution

Opposite:
Aditi is the ancient Sanskrit word for "abundance" and "creative power," and is also the name of one of the most ancient goddesses—the mother of all gods on earth. This image of the earth goddess, which is also the symbol of the exhibition, was discovered in Madhya Pradesh in the heart of the Indian subcontinent and dates to about 1500 B.C.

Contents

Foreword

Rajeev Sethi, the talented creator and driving force behind the *Aditi* exhibit, has developed an extraordinary sympathy and understanding of young and old alike in the traditional cultures of India and by the very process of exposing them has revealed how essentially complex and fascinating they are. The people of India as a whole have a kind of unanimity in their essence imbued by elaborate performance, ceremony, and custom. As we know, the Vedic-Aryan culture of ancient India still dominates most of the land, but earlier and later cultures are interwoven into this fabric. Even though the Hindu culture is twenty-five hundred or more years old, the influence of Muslim life, history, and culture is ever present. The Moghul Empire made its mark on the country as a whole in a manner which will not soon be forgotten. It is a pity, at least to this author, that the principles enunciated by Akbar and seen in the architecture of Fatehpur Sikri have somehow failed to catch up to the present time. Those principles simply attempted to express in architecture the fact that India as a whole should be united and not divided for communal reasons.

In the world today, we note that communalism is dominant again and that the age-old religious fundamentals of the different sects and castes are still ever present. *Aditi* celebrates the perpetuation of underlying currents which will probably never die out in India and which serve to strengthen and perpetuate values within the culture which are strong and positive. This may well be founded on religious ethics, for ethics, as differentiated from blind faith, are always to be preserved and admired. The demonstrations of skills and crafts by the people whose culture *Aditi* pervades reveal timeless truths and continue to fascinate and intrigue the viewer. This is part of the age-old India that we think about and admire without knowing very much about it. The fact that Mr. Sethi has developed a technique of demonstrating the realities of this culture is exceptional and something that should be admired, and we should persevere in our attempts to understand the variety that remains in the world today.

During my own life I have experienced India in many phases, beginning from my childhood to today. I have always felt an essential peace and harmony in Indian village life. To me, the sight of children squatting at play outside of small houses in the sun is a perennial indication of peace and quietness. May such vistas which persist in my mind persist also forever in this fascinating and diverse country, which presents in its rural life an extraordinary tapestry of customs and culture that we can only admire.

S. Dillon Ripley

Chairman
American National Committee
for the Festival of India

Secretary Emeritus
Smithsonian Institution

Snuggled safely in a basket
high above the road, this
child accompanies his
mother to work.

Preface

When *Aditi* was first conceived seven years ago, we were determined to change the prevailing pursuit of culture as a leisure-time activity. Nor did we find the customary presentation of Indian art as it relates to the study of schools, styles, and chronology a particularly illuminating exercise.

As *Aditi* created itself, the canvas for it stretched on its own. The chosen theme of the rites of passage (*samskāra*) unfolds the pattern of this culture we call Indian. It is an integral pattern. Making, being, and expressing are the same things, so that the reason, or the specific occasion is an event on which its own artifacts, related functional skills, supportive traditions, or rituals converge. Conventional boundaries between theater, craft, music, dance, drama, poetry appear to disappear. Supportive relationships are emphasized.

The theme of *Aditi* is simple: It is joy in life that is best expressed through the desire for new life, life expressing itself as an expansion of a seed into the ongoing spiral of experience.

Aditi traces the cycle of time itself from the abundant desire for life (and that which precedes desire) to the point when life again furthers life, spinning off into yet another cycle.

The cycle contracts itself into the child's world. No individual or community so wholly reveals its nature and its essential values as in its relation to its children. For the child is the repository of our collective experiences, our hopes, and the imbalances between them—what we conceive the ideal man or ideal woman to be. A child then is both child and adult, in capsule.

Aditi presents what it has to say by drawing on a cluster of fundamentally Indian metaphors.

The Indian aphorism, "Yat pinde tatso brahmānde"—'In microcosm lies the macrocosm'—is manifested in the fact that a potter is also called *prajāpati*, the progenitor. His equipment and action are symbolic of the cosmic forces of creation. The potter's wheel is Vishnu's *chakra*, the wheel of eternal law, according to which everything proceeds into manifestation and is again withdrawn from it; the stick for turning the wheel is Indra'a *vajra*, thunderbolt; the flat cone of clay is Shiva's *linga* or phallic form, and the water container is the *kūndā* of Brahmā, a symbol of the mendicant ascetic. This consciousness is invoked in a dedication to the potter's wheel, *chāk pūjā*, that is required to solemnize weddings in northern India. The pot is also a form of the goddess in many parts of India, as of the human body in Kabir's poetry. It comes into its own when finally cut from the spinning mound of clay with a piece of string—the ritual thread of initiation—*janāyupavīt*.

While reflecting a strong local and regional flavor, *Aditi* highlights the presence of a collective vitality that has its own built-in symmetries. The subsistence of this vitality is rich in myth, symbol, and song—in ritual and reticences that are older than thinking.

The bird, harbinger of spring, invokes fertility. The parrot—*vāhana*, vehicle of Kāmdeva, the God of Love—and the fish—the banner of his consort, Manmathā—appear in the memory of a craftsperson as symbols appropriate to a marriage. The *jadao* pendant, prepared for the bridal trousseau (discreetly enamelled on the reverse side to prevent the gold from wearing off against the skin) signals the same belief with parrots engraved intricately on a tree of life. This courtly interpretation of the craftsmen's blessings has an echo in the classical traditions more than a thousand miles away in the south, where *killi mālai*, a garland of parrots, is symbolized by a parrot on a pin placed on the shoulder of the goddess Mīnākshī.

When viewed in its entirety, India is bewilderingly diverse. But these varied traditions merge or influence each other, the rural and tribal vernacular traditions interacting with the unbroken classical traditions. The traditions of microcommunities of itinerant artisans, who have been forced to move with the imperative of employment, combine with the tales and songs of the traveling bards and performers to help unify this varied whole.

Like the potter at his wheel, we have tried to place the object and the skill (through demonstration wherever possible) in its context (the marriage). We then go further to suggest the link between the object and the maker and its contemporary usage.

The rituals that *Aditi* documents illustrate how early and contemporary man attempts to control and understand a mysterious environment and render it tangible through symbols, images, and sounds. These rituals reinforce interpersonal, family, and community relationships and customs. Wherever possible, this exhibit reveals them in the light of contemporary sensibilities and, in some instances, in the context of the deterioration of tradition, the disparity of economic pursuits and achievements, and the influence of a mass media and an "official" culture that profoundly affects the way people perceive and express themselves.

For instance, the worship of *Ahoi Ashtamī*, performed by mothers for the safety and protection of their children, is now merely a ritual among urban mothers, who continue to observe it in a perfunctory manner. They stick a printed sheet on the distempered wall and, for a small moment in a day, urge their children to observe the *pūjā* (wor-

A ritual vessel for carrying sacred Ganges water, this *kamandalu* or *kūndā* is decorated with leafy fronds that symbolize new life springing from the waters.

Kamandalu. 19th century. Brass, 11 x 8″ (29 x 20 cm). Collection of C.L. Bharany, New Delhi.

ship). No doubt cement walls do not lend themselves to clay relief, and who has time or inclination to mess about in mud anyway? But the communication between the mother and child so delicately enshrined in the eight-day ritual continues to need a vehicle for expression.

Similarly, the potter has stopped making some votives because there is no longer a felt need, and the worship of Shītalā Mātā, the goddess of smallpox, takes on different functions within the reality of modern medicine.

A man driving a tractor and using factory-made fertilizers does not need the same foot-wear and the same plow as his forebears.

Women who once sang songs on their way to the well, sharing the day's happenings with each other, have now at some places, merely to open a tap in their backyard. Good. No doubt the songs may die—the pot may change—but what is replacing that energy?

Children continue to learn, albeit in the absence of time-tested informal education that nurtures the wit and wisdom of ages; community experiences and folk customs that range from means of recreation to ballads and stories of timeless value have been replaced by bookish knowledge, often of dubious quality. Young men and women continue to sing, but most film music, it seems to me, cannot teach them as much about human relationships as their own songs and ballads, now slipping from oral memory.

Much of the material culture and oral tradition is disappearing, except for that which is preserved in museums and academic institutions. But this record remains relatively inaccessible to those who need it most, since the breakdown of kinship structures and social interaction has seriously challenged the tradition of oral instruction. In the face of modern stimuli, artisans no longer practice the oral traditions that preserved their culture for so many generations.

The potters, weavers, and leather craftsmen, whose sons want to leave the profession due to social intimidation, no longer know how to tell the tales of Bhakt Ravidās and Sant Kabir (widely popular saints who belonged to the castes of the craftsmen), or to explain the origin of the title "prajāpat."

Many artisans are still not aware of new or some of the old products that they can make, modify, or easily develop to meet new needs. They are unaware of each other's ingenuity and often have no access to the finest available demonstration in their own skills. Sitting in their isolated workshops they are, so to speak, re-inventing the wheel. Some useful skills that have been lost in one region have been revived or are still in existence in another. Lost techniques and broken-down sympathies need to be shared and given a new life.

Women at a community well in Rajasthan draw water that first is blessed by the gods and goddesses carved on the interior of the well. As they pull the heavy pots and in time with the squeaky pulleys, they sing songs to each other to ease their work.

Traditional wall decorations frame a collage of contemporary snapshots of movie stars and famous singers.

Although designs for better kilns may diminish the potter's risk, they do not necessarily alter his reverence for the tool. Any visitor to a modern factory in India will observe little shrines and sacred markings on steel and plastic equipment even though the deeper significance of the worship of Vishwakarmā, the God of Arts and Crafts, is hardly remembered.

Most of what *Aditi* presents is still part of a living tradition in India, or that which is within easy recall. The concept informing the selection of objects in this exhibit and their display was based on several considerations.

In some sections, objects and performance demonstrations of certain regions predominate to focus attention on the way a given place and people relate to a given situation. Of necessity, the choice of these regions has been somewhat arbitrary.

Different regions of the country continue to express themselves elaborately—or less elaborately—in different rites and customs, some readily lending themselves to examination by outsiders.

In some cases, a traditional skill has been applied in such non-traditional display formats, as the Mithilā marriage and the *vadakappa* ceremony for pregnant women. These thematic presentations have been produced specially for *Aditi* by craftsmen familiar with the theme, after considerable dialogue. Those included in the exhibit have been carefully differentiated from the traditional items and skills that have remained unchanged for centuries.

While the potters of Molela even today draw their main sustenance from the making of votive plaques and shrines, there is also a moment, a rhythm, in their existence, when they reflect upon and express what they see around them, including motorcars and aeroplanes. This effort may not evoke the same *dhyān* (a kind of concentration) as more traditional creations, yet making the mural "Fair Time" for *Aditi* helped the Molela craftsmen amuse themselves and cater to the child—their own or the one in them.

This absorption of contemporary metaphor is apparent in all vital and virile traditions. The moment of fusion between skill and insight occurs in the traditional craftsman's mind very much as it would in that of an artist anywhere, anytime. Still, traditional craftsmen have developed an unusual capacity to merge simple beauty with a high standard of functionality. For them, the creative process is often private, detached, and anonymous. Although expanding markets, official or scholarly patronage, or the lack of it, can distract, as it can alternatively energize or leave no mark, there are as many variables as there are craftsmen and circumstances.

Creative expression has also flourished under the pressure of commercial demands, although this may lead to a dismaying tendency toward change for its own sake. At the same time, this pressure can also lead to renewed vigor, innovation, and an extension of the tradition. The Mithilā women today may produce on paper pictures by the hundreds for a large, undiscerning clientele (like the proverbial terra cotta Mickey Mouse made by rural potters for tourists), but their new-found material comfort and status give these craftswomen the time and freedom to seek out and savor the perfection that arises from continuity with the traditional idiom. It is also true that in Mithilā today there are many more women and even men (which was previously unthinkable) who have taken to the brush. There is a temporary boom, a frenzied euphoria, but the finest survive.

While emphasizing the contemporary applications of these skills as a versatile vocabulary, we have also chosen to display items of somewhat dubious influences where the eye has chosen without the mind or its continuity and viceversa. These have been placed side by side with objects from museums, objects that reflect an unbroken lineage, objects produced by virtue of skills that have slipped into non-use but could perhaps be revived or are being revived, objects created for export by international designers who recognize traditional skills as a means of expressing different sensibilities, objects that will perhaps never find their way into a museum and yet articulate a fine moment from a living community.

The real relevance of the old values is in the inspiration they provide for the present. We do not worship the past for the sake of history. In our critical analysis, we reveal the imaginative skill of the artisans to show the nature of insight that leads to the process of renewal, growth, and progress from the old to the new tools. The earth has been plowed for hundreds of years, even as the water has been drawn and used for a variety of needs that have not changed. But methods have evolved in each age, with man at the center effecting change and making the most from his knowledge of resources.

Look at the patched-up quilt—a *gudrī*, in the making of which is invoked the presence of a deity, Chithāriya mā, the Lady of the Tatters (an observation I owe to Stella Kramrisch). In it is enshrined the holistic Indian concept that all parts belong to the whole and must return to it. The faqīrs or mendicants dressed in little rags or tatters and the songs of the jogīs, itinerant bards, reinforce the wisdom of this idea, while the lady who stitches it is the evidence of traditional common-sense inherent in doing more with less.

The arts and crafts displayed in *Aditi* tell the story of this struggle of the human family as a supremely resourceful unit of nature whose future depends upon their will to make themselves.

Puppet of Man Plowing. *Contemporary. Painted leather, 25 x 2" (65 x 5 cm). Chitrakala Parishad, Bangalore.*

Rajeev Sethi
New Delhi, India
June 1985

Acknowledgements

Foremost, I wish to acknowledge the anonymous genius of India's artisans and performers without whose active participation an exhibition of the dimension of *Aditi—A Celebration of Life* would not have been possible. Likewise, I wish to acknowledge the invaluable contribution of Mrs. Pupul Jayakar, chairman of the Indian Advisory Committee for the Festival of India. An exhibition as complex as *Aditi* could never have been conceived or implemented without her visionary guidance and support. Under her extraordinary leadership, several departments of the Government of India have come together during the remarkable joint effort of organizing *Aditi*.

Aditi, as it is presented in the United States today, owes the success of its development to the constant support of Dr. Kapila Vatsyayan and S. K. Misra of the Festival of India Committee, to Natwar Singh, formerly of the office of External Affairs of the Government of India, to Shiromani Sharma, development commissioner (Handicrafts), to Diljeet Aurora and P. Shankar of The Handicrafts & Handlooms Export Corporation, to Niranjan Desai and Vijay Singh as coordinators of the Festival, to Nani Mittal and Pallavi Shah of Air-India, and to Dr. Jyotindra Jain, director of the Crafts Museum in New Delhi who arranged the loan of objects from museums throughout India. The presence, involvement, and scholarship of M. N. Deshpande has been a constant source of strength to all who worked with him. His rare ability to bring out the best in everyone made the teamwork required for *Aditi* a most joyous experience. I must also thank Probir Guha, Narpat Singh Rathore, and Madan Lal for their work with the performers, and Amar Nath Khanna and A. L. Lumba for their tireless assistance.

In America, all Indians owe to Dr. Stella Kramrisch their immense gratitude, for, through her work she opened the doors to an appreciation of India's rural and ritual arts which were little known before the 1960s. I also wish to thank S. Dillon Ripley, secretary emeritus of the Smithsonian Institution and chairman of the American National Committee for the Festival of India, for his constant concern and warm support of *Aditi*. His deep love of South Asia has manifested itself in many ways throughout his most distinguished career. I wish to thank as well Mr. Ripley's successor as secretary, Robert McCormick Adams, and the Institution's Board of Regents for their interest in the exhibition and sensitive consideration of its needs. The support of John Jameson, the Institution's assistant secretary for administration, and Ann Leven, its treasurer, has been crucial for *Aditi* and must be acknowledged here. Also, I would like to thank Senator Daniel Patrick Moynihan and Mrs. Liz Moynihan for always being ready and willing to assist on this project; and Dorothy Norman whose love and knowledge of India always provides one with fresh insights.

For their encouragement, I would like to thank the Ambassador of India to the United States Mr. K. Shankar Bajpai and Mrs. Meera Bajpai; and for making me see the practical way my good friends Naresh and Madhu Trehan.

Of course, *Aditi* could never have been brought to the United States were it not for the unwavering attention of several individuals, who have nurtured the idea of bringing this exhibition to America for the last six years. At the Smithsonian, I am indebted to Charles Blitzer who, when he was assistant secretary for history and art, first saw in *Aditi* a vehicle for joyous and creative dialogue and who created the impetus that has, in fact, made *Aditi* possible; to Ralph Rinzler who actively pursued bringing *Aditi* to the United States with his characteristic instinct for cross-cultural exchange; and to Jeffrey LaRiche, without whom all the good intentions and good will for *Aditi* may never have found a constructive channeling. At the Indo-U.S. Subcommission on Education and Culture, I am grateful for the unflagging assistance and encouragement of Ted Tanen and Patrice Fusillo who, with all their nationwide responsibilities for the Festival of India, never forgot *Aditi*. Also, my thanks go to Lora Redford, formerly of the Subcommission, who has continued her interest in this project since its inception.

It is a pleasure to acknowledge those who have joined the Smithsonian and the Government of India in providing financial support, and they are Air-India, the Armand Hammer Foundation, UNICEF (United Nations Children's Fund), the Chicago Pneumatic Tool Company, and the Indo-U.S. Subcommission on Education and Culture. We are most grateful for their generous assistance. At the Smithsonian, I would like to acknowledge the Foreign Currency Program of the Office of Fellowships and Grants which has made available important funds for the exhibition. Within that office, Francine Berkowitz and Jackie Rand have provided excellent advice and counsel. I also wish to thank the contributing members of the Smithsonian, the Office of Contributing Membership, and its director, Janet Fesler, for their support of this volume; and the Women's Committee of the Smithsonian Associates for its support of the educational packet that will accompany the exhibition. Finally, this project could never have been sustained were it not for the Ford Foundation, which provided the support to me for the original research on *Aditi* prior to its installation in the United Kingdom in 1982.

Many individuals within and outside the Smithsonian have helped in the preparation of the exhibition and its accompanying book and to all I extend my most heartfelt thanks. Unfortunately, space does not allow a complete listing of all who have contributed along the way. I would nevertheless like to thank those whose help comes most readily to mind.

At the Smithsonian's National Museum of Natural History, I wish to thank its director, Richard Fiske, for giving *Aditi* a home in America, and thank as well Larry O'Reilly, Sheila Mutchler, Marge Stoller, Laura McKie, Kate Rinzler, Susan Voss, Constance Lee, and Chip Clark, all of whom attended to the never-ending details surrounding such a large exhibition. I also wish to acknowledge the fine skill of Beth Miles, formerly of this museum, who designed *Aditi*'s installation and maintained her wonderful humor throughout our collaboration; and the dedication of Rochelle Kessler, who worked ceaselessly with me in New Delhi to coordinate most of the on-site aspects of this complicated project.

Performers and craft demonstrators are as integral to *Aditi* as is the display of objects. The staff of the Smithsonian Office of Folklife Programs, under its director Peter Seitel, managed the concerns of the participants with rare sensitivity and accomplishment. In particular, I wish to thank Richard Kurin, Jonathan Mark Kenoyer, and Nita Kumar for their masterful organization and care for the participants; Daphne Shuttleworth for her thoughtful and imaginative design for this book; and Arlene Liebenau for her generous assistance with the book's manuscript.

I wish to thank the staff of the Smithsonian Institution Press, but in particular the book's editor, Patricia Gallagher, and its picture editor, Frances C. Rowsell, who approached this project with keen sensibilities and wonderful dedication. And assignment photographers Chip Clark and Jyoti Rath provided many of the wonderful photographs that make this book so special. At the Freer Gallery of Art, Dr. Milo Beach was always available to provide invaluable advice on both the exhibit and the book. Of course, I also must acknowledge the authors of the book: Ms. Pria Devi, Dr. Nazir Jairazbhoy, Dr. Sudhir Kakar, Dr. Stella Kramrisch, Dr. Richard Kurin, and Dr. Wendy Doniger O'Flaherty, and consultant, Dr. Jonathan Mark Kenoyer. To them, all readers of this volume owe their gratitude for careers spent illuminating this vast, provocative, and too little understood realm of Indian culture.

At the Smithsonian's Museum Shops and Mail Order Catalogue offices, I wish to acknowledge the important contribution of the staff of talented merchandisers—Samuel Greenberg, Donald Press, Josephine Rowan, Kathy Borrus, Lisa Wanderman and Meredith Rinaldi. They have brought knowledge of traditional Indian skills to a wider public than could be reached solely by an exhibition and a book, as well as concrete benefit to the craftsmen of India.

Several individuals have helped to nurture this project in subtle ways too numerous to document. I appreciate greatly the constant attention given *Aditi* by Mary Lynne McElroy, Andrew McCoy, and Carol Anderson of the Smithsonian Office of Public Service; and the attention of Cheryl Brauner, Saundra Thomas, Richard Conroy, Brian LeMay, and Kennedy Schmertz of the Directorate of International Activities. At the Office of Exhibits Central, I wish to acknowledge the contribution of John Widener who travelled to India to hold workshops on the packing and crating of museum objects and brought with him the experience of 27 years at the Smithsonian.

In London, I wish to thank Madhu Khanna for her camaraderie; and Robert Skelton, keeper of the India Department at the Victoria and Albert Museum, and Geoffrey de Bellaigue, surveyor of the Queen's Works of Arts, for their support in lending objects from their magnificent collections.

And finally, in India, there are so many individuals and institutions without whose support *Aditi* could never have been organized and sent abroad. I owe them all an immense debt of gratitude which I can never appropriately acknowledge. The following list is a symbolic tribute to their extraordinary contribution.

Rās Līlā—the circular dance of life beneath the autumn full moon. Playing his magical flute Krishna enlivens the universe and as the milkmaids dance, he appears before each one, a companion in the dance of life.

Introduction

Aditi is a riddle. Like the Sun, she is also fire as energy. Awakened, she is the first dancer. As the active transforming principle she becomes operative through nature's immutable laws, the flux of time, and the ceaseless flow of seasons. Playfully she weaves a circular path, turning around, by the very movement creating cyclic time, ensuring passage. As the prime mover, Aditi, the central node of energy, is also the crucible for the senses undifferentiated. Activated, they manifest as sound, touch, sight, taste, and fragrance, in turn invoking space, air, fire, water, and earth.

Certain imperatives determine Aditi's manifestations and directions. In her ascending tendency Aditi follows the northern journey of the sun into the constellation of Makara, the crocodile, a period of longer days and shorter nights, a time for sowing and harvesting, for abundance and fertility—creating art that expresses itself through energy contained in symbols of the auspicious, drawn on floor and wall, through brilliant sun-dyed colors of garments, through song, dance, mime, and riddle.

In the descending tendency she enters the southern journey of the sun, into the constellation of Karka, the crab. This is a period of longer nights and shorter days, when the gods sleep, the earth lies fallow, and all auspicious rites and ceremonies end. It is a time for the propitiation of the malevolent forces of nature, sorcery, and disease, for assuaging the cry for protection that echoes from a time without beginning through the recitation of spells, the drawing of magical geometric abstractions on floor and wall, and through ritual gestures and rites of protection.

From the soaring snow peaks of the Himalayas and their flower-swept valleys in the north, to the rain forests on the southernmost shores of an ocean-cradled India, from the pronged Ganges delta in the east to the deserts of the west, a cultural commonality unifies the land mass, transcending changing landscape and climate and ethnographic variation.

An ancient cultural geography familiar from the Purāna texts reveals a unifying vision that reaches out to the cardinal directions to establish the sacred ground of pilgrimage and the sites of fairs and festivals at the confluence of rivers, on mountain peaks, on sea shores, and in the midst of dense forests, thus creating an ethos of the pathways, of moving feet of pilgrim and traveler. With this there exists an oral tradition of singing and traveling; the mendicant, *kathā vāchak*, the story teller, and picture showman, the bard, the juggler, the acro-

A fiery sun, modeled in clay on the wall of a rural home, invokes the god Sūrya to energize growth in plants, animals, and man.

25

bat and the *bahrūpiyā*, the actor who mimes the roles of goddess and hero.

This landscape of movement and an oral literature ensure within a traditional framework continuous transformation—a process of learning, absorbing, creating, and teaching that establishes the cultural unity, the ground of India. From this flows the ocean of story, the landscape of the epics and Purānic legends; out of this are born image and icon, rites and rituals, fairs and festivals.

Three vast religious, sociological, and cultural rivers met and mingled in the heartlands of India. The most archaic and the most pristine were the food gatherers, claiming to be the first-born of the earth, the original inhabitants of this land, claiming descent from Shiva, the first ancestor, with his links to earth and fertility, to death and life.

Tribes who dwelt in forest, mountain, and cave until fifty years ago practiced *beawar*, a shifting agriculture, refusing to wound the Earth Mother with the plow. These people perceived themselves as living in an intimate kinship with animals and trees, with stone and water, sustaining a living tradition that nurtured the belief through enactment of the ritual—through dance, song, or liturgic drawing. The energy thus awakened was not dissipated or dispersed, but rather ensured its own fulfillment.

As they approach the twenty-first century; these tribes are slowly losing their sense of wonder and joy, their insights into nature and the sacred; they are leaving their habitats to be absorbed into surrounding villages and changing their artifacts, tools, skills, and entertainments.

The second stream was that of nomadic tribes, the wanderers of the earth who centuries earlier entered India, the land of rivers, in search of pastures. These people had an intense visual and aural vocabulary of color, light, and sound; an art that was transient, that moved with cattle along river bank and through forest; and the swiftness of eye and ear born of moving landscape.

These tribes were cattle rearers and original horse riders whose ballads of love and elopement created gods in their own male and heroic likeness, with the horse and rider as the symbol of the hero king and divinity and rooted pillars as uprising symbols of virility and power. It is from their pastoral culture of tree, flower, bird, and animal, with an ear tuned to the bells of cows returning home at dusk, that the Krishna myth emerged, to be woven into painting, song, circular dances, and mime, to be taken by performers to the vast countryside where, under the flowering trees of mango, *Krishna chūrā*, *kadamba*, and tamarind the legend of Krishna is reenacted and thus given life and immediacy.

Embellished with figures of human couples, *mithuna*, and growing plants, this elaborate water pot depicts the power of fertility in the sacred water that will be carried in it.

Ritual Pot. *19th century. Brass, 2 x 2" (5¼ x 5¼ cm). Collection of O.P. Jain, New Delhi.*

On the day after Dīwālī, devout Vaishnavas in city and village cook and offer *annakūt*, a mountain of food of every conceivable variety, to the divine child. Songs, dances, lights, and flowers transform village and home. In pastoral communities of the north, the *Govardhan pūjā* is the vernacular version of the more sophisticated *annakūt*. In this nomadic culture, men mold massive images out of cowdung, which constitutes the first pile of cowdung cakes to form the Govardhan hill—the hill which Krishna raised with his little finger to protect the people Vrindāvan along with their herds from the torrential rain sent by the angry Indra.

Rooted in the Earth, stable, a settled culture and society had emerged, already mature and ancient five thousand years ago. These agricultural societies with their craft technologies, myths, rites, and rituals were interspersed among mushrooming cities. Both the classical, *mārgī*, and the vernacular, *deshī*, coexisted in this culture; the chacolithic technologies have survived alongside the machines of modern industry; ancient myths are performed for television broadcasts. A comprehension that culture is never static, but in constant movement, recreating itself by constant absorption of the new, however alien or heretical, has enabled the survival of core perceptions and rituals—the Vedic, tantric and the *vrata* observances of the woman.

Integral to these societies were male-oriented artisan guilds, with their knowledge of material, tool, and skill. Fulfilling the functional needs of city, religious center, and village community, craftsmen carved the massive stone temples based on detailed instructions found in the Shilpa Shāstras, the Hindu scriptures that instruct the artist and the craftsman; from the same guilds came the stone masons who carved in village tribal society hero or *satī* stones to the ancestors. A total anonymity of name, of craftsman and creator, are characteristic of this tradition, yet it does not lack vigor and clarity of expression.

But a peoples' culture of the creative, not touched by the rigid authority of the sacred scriptures, the Shāstras, had taken root in the countryside, where woman, the shaman, and the poet wove a multidimensional culture of song, dance, incantation, molding of icon, and drawing of magical diagram.

Samskāra rites based on a Brāhmanic liturgy, rites of initiation and transformation exist today, providing milestones in the life of a caste Hindu; each initiation, like the serpent sloughing its old skin, is regarded as birth and a beginning.

The first samskāra is the *garbha yonī*, the birth from the womb. The second is the *dwija janma* or *upanayana*. In this ritual, death and rebirth are both enacted. The disciple entering a new life of the *brahmāchārī*, or student disciple, undergoes ceremonies addressed to the

This geometrical design, called an *aripan*, represents the cosmos as a bamboo grove—an illustration of fertility and family life— which grows up around an ancestor like a clump of bamboo around the first shoot.

dead, such as shaving of the head and paring of nails. The beginning, the rebirth, is enacted in the recitation of the secret *gāyatrī mantra* invoking the sun, whispered into the ear by father to son, and the wearing of the sacred handspun thread across the shoulders. The recitation of the mantra demands accurate enunciation and the emphasis given to certain words to give magical power to the incantation.

The third initiation in the life of the householder is the *trija janma*, the third birth, or *amrit yoni*, the birth into nectar, in which the *guru* symbolically takes the disciple or *sanyāsī* seeking wisdom into his belly and holds him in darkness for three days and three nights, after which the disciple emerges from darkness as young and luminous as the Sun; the gods gather to witness this presencing.

At the samskāra rites of death and the later *shrāddha*, or rites to the ancestors, that follow, the roles are reversed; it is now the son who releases his father's or mother's spirit from the body, chanting mantras and lighting the pyre as he circumambulates his parent's mortal remains.

A substratum of female memories of power and energy, independent of Brāhmanic samskāra rites, provides an umbilical cord that links woman to the farthest limits of time, when primordial maternal rights and control of power, energy, and wisdom prevailed. The India of today recognizes Shakti as primal energy, female in form and attribute, the guardian of mysteries and rites of initiation. The mother is the channel for communicating these secrets of word and ritual to her daughter, thus making them vivid and contemporary and ensuring their continuity.

The women of Mithilā, when questioned on this archaic knowledge and secret wisdom, speak of it as *parampara*—"we hold it from a time without beginning, we carry it in our wombs."

In the rites of initiation which are integral to this secret teaching are those that surround birth, puberty, marriage, and childbirth. *Kumārī vrata, gaurī pūjā,* Gangor worship, the Yama Pukar *vrata* propitiate those mysteries concerned with puberty, marriage, and a rich fruiting. In the vigorous vrata culture that surrounds these rituals, symbols of bamboo, the plantain tree, the lotus, and the bird and sun-dried clay icons of the female, emphasizing sex and fertility, are delineated on floor or wall or on the body of the girl; they also decorate the walls of the nuptial chamber. The symbolism is delicate, suggestive, never overstated, but comprehensible because of the commonality of symbol, perception, and heritage.

In a creation myth common to the countryside the Ādi shakti, the primordial ever-young goddess, spins the threads of creation. As she conceives and creates, she, in turn, is vanquished by the male gods who are born of her; she passes to them the power that ensures her own destruction, for she conveys the wisdom that in *srishti*, or creation, is the seed or *bīja* of *samhar*, or destruction. In such a scenario of ending and beginning, death is an ending and yet a passage to a beginning. In *srishti bīja* is the *samhar bīja*; in *samhar* is the *srishti*.

Pupul Jayakar
Chairman
Indian Advisory Committee
for the Festival of India

A tradition passed down from mother to daughter is revealed in the intricate paintings of Ganga Devi of Mithilā.

Aditi– A Celebration of Life

Pria Devi and Richard Kurin

Aditi is sky, Aditi is earth,
Aditi is mother, father and son.
Aditi is the five kinds of all men who are.
Aditi is all that has been born and shall be.
("Hymn to the Cosmic Gods," Rig Veda
1:89:10)[1]

A four-handed goddess of fertility and abundance, carrying bowls of sweets in her outstretched right hands. In her front left hand, she holds a bowl of vegetables, while the one behind bears an image that offers protection to the devotees.

Fertility Goddess. *Contemporary. Papier mâché, 20½ x 10½" (8 x 4 cm). Collection of Pupul Jayakar, New Delhi.*

Aditi is originally the mother of the solar gods, revered by the Indo-Aryans who settled in northern India and first began to sing her praises around 1500 to 1200 B.C. Like many other gods and goddesses who predate those of contemporary Hinduism, her characteristics seem at once awesome and contradictory to Western eyes.

Aditi is female, androgyne, and is
    sometimes addressed as male.
She is the heifer, and so animal.
She is cosmic, and domestic.
She is benevolence itself, yet is also a
    battle goddess.
She pervades, ubiquitously, like space itself.
And in time she devours her own creation.[2]

Who, or what then is Aditi?

Aditi is the source, the process, and the essence of life itself. Aditi unifies beginnings and endings, man and woman, nature and the gods. In this, the concept of Aditi poses a challenge to our usual linear way of thinking, forcing us instead to think in terms of cycles. Consider that Aditi is also called "Uttanapad" the crouching goddess, and is depicted with her legs spread in the stance associated with both *yoga* and the act of giving birth. She is described simultaneously as the mother and the daughter of Daksha—hence the paradox of mutual creation: the parent creating and being created by the child.

The exhibition *Aditi* celebrates the life cycle starting from fertility and the coming of age through courtship, betrothal, marriage, conception, pregnancy, birth, infancy, childhood and maturation to the point when life again furthers life, initiating yet another cycle. In the exhibition each stage of life is informed by the ritual designs, traditional paintings, craftwork, folk songs, dances, stories, and activities associated with it in India.

In India, many of the samskāras, or rites which mark the life cycle, have as their aim the generation, transformation, and perfection of the child. In keeping with this, the exhibition highlights and has special significance for children. It is to them that our knowledge, skills, and dreams are conveyed. And it is only through them that life is propagated and becomes truly cyclical.

Aditi,
Housewife, goddess and sky womb of ancient
   sun gods,
Says of herself,
*"This is the ancient and accepted pathway by which
All gods have come into existence."*
("Hymn of Indra," Rig Veda 4:18:1)[3]

The *Aditi* exhibition also stresses the role crafts-people, artisans, musicians, dancers, and itinerant performers play in the life cycle. Parents like artists share with the goddess the power of creating. For parents, out of a moment's secret happiness comes a new human being. Their "creation," the child, laughs and cries and grows and plays. It suffers, it experiences, it begins to know. In its turn it learns to do, to make, to give birth. What mystery is this, from a drop of water and a pinch of dust?

Out of grass or clay, wood, fiber or molten metal comes a toy, utensil or a ritual object. From sound comes music and song, from body movement, dance and acrobatics. These "creations" are felt by people and bring with them laughter and tears, new experiences, knowledge, entertainment, and inspiration.

Every village and old town in India has its ancient trees, its sleeping pond, and its shrines. So too, within its maze of alleyways, does it have its artisans' quarters. There, people as well as objects are crafted. Each craftsman, each artisan, each musician, by the very act of making, puts some-thing new into being. And in this art itself, passed from father to son, or mother to daughter, is recalled the ancient, yet familiar way of Aditi.

I. Fertility

Catch oh brother,
Catch the big fish
Where the sun meets the moon
At the coming together of the three rivers.
(A song of the Bauls, itinerant singers and
wandering mystics of Bengal)[4]

You are entering another country. India.

It is as much a geography of the mind and its
senses as that of a land and its rivers.

Consider the very earth and the sky and the
moment they converge.

Above you the open Indian sky, tautened to
white with the hot summer sun, is as abstract and
relentless as truth itself. The supportive earth lies
red, black, white, lion-colored, and rippling; intimate to us; moist or parched; in several odors and
scents. It multiplies and it feeds. Now it waits
breathlessly. The sky darkens. It lowers. Then,
charged and thundering, it meets the earth in a
violent life-giving rain.

Fertility as the potent, creative power animating
all life cycles is common to plants, animals,
humans, and gods.

By just one single seed
Alone that sprouts
Into a mighty tree,
That's how worlds begin . . . .
(Attributed to Tukā Rām, the householder
mystic and shopkeeper saint of Maharashtra,
seventeenth century)[5]

A farmer and his sons prepare
the plowed field for planting
in anticipation of the life-giving
monsoon rain.

Overleaf: Shiva and Pārvatī
on Mount Kailāsha, shown
sitting on a tiger-skin in
amorous embrace. *Benares
Hindu University, Bharat Kala
Bhavan.*

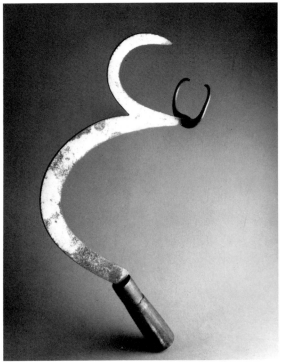

Among the Nilgiri hill
tribes of Tamil Nadu in
south India, the figure of
the buffalo represents male
virility. These pottery figurines are fertility symbols
on burial urns from the
megalithic period in south
India, c. 1st millennium B.C.

Lids for Pottery Burial
Object. *Mid-1st millennium
B.C. Terra cotta; (left) 9 x
4³⁄₄"; (23¹⁄₄ x 12¹⁄₄ cm),
(right) 7³⁄₄ x 6 x 8¹⁄₂" (20 x
15¹⁄₂ x 22 cm). Government
Museum, Madras.*

The ritual iron sickle,
made by Kota ironworkers
of the Nilgiri region, bears
the auspicious horns of the
buffalo, which is sacrificed
for the fertility of the fields
and the well-being of the
herds.

Decorated Sickle. *Contemporary. Steel and wood,
13¹⁄₄ x 9" (35 x 23¹⁄₂ cm).
Government Museum,
Madras.*

The *gagarā* or water pot is
also an important symbol
of fertility because it holds
the vital fluid essential to
all life.

The tree as a symbol of fertility and protection is seen in all contexts of Indian life and art. Above, the great banyan tree at Shivpur, Calcutta, illustrates the continual circulation of energy. Though the main trunk crumbled long ago, the ever-extending branches and roots still provide shade and protection.

The seed is both the beginning and the end of the crop. The earth provides a nurturing field within which it grows. The seed, represented as male, and the field, represented as female, are popular symbols of fertility in Indian thought. The bounty of life-providing harvests is made possible by the fertility of seed and field. The successfully harvested crop staves off the threat of widespread famine, sickness, and death for yet another season. Food is also at the root of the social order. It is the unit of value and exchange in the traditional village economy and hence provides the basis for rural agricultural society. Given the significance of successful agriculture, the sprout, water, and even its container, the womb-like earthen water jar, are greatly revered.

The Dalliance of Rādhā
and Krishna under the
Kadamba Tree. *Contempo-*
rary. Grass work, 20 x 14"
(51 x 36 cm). HHEC, New
Delhi.

The ascetic Shiva, is seen meditating in the forest attended by Nandī.

Shiva and the Ganges. *18th century. Indian miniature. Alwar Museum, Alwar, Rajasthan.*

Below: Gangā Mātā, Mother Ganges. All rivers flow into the sacred Ganges providing nourishment for the soil and nourishment for the soul.

In Indian thought, the fertility inherent in nature is animated by the fertility of the gods. In post-Vedic Hindu thought, macrocosmic fertility is represented by the reproductive energy or *shakti* of the goddess Pārvatī and her consort, the god Shiva. It is their creative power, often represented as the union of divine *yonī* (womb) and *linga* (phallus), that forms the world. So potent is godly power that heavenly water from the hair of Shiva forms the great river Ganges. Fertility is commonly invoked through the icons of gods and goddesses, either individually—in the case of a mother goddess—or in a conjoined male and female pair. Godly fertility may be represented in plant and animal forms. The fish, the turtle, the water snake, and the fully opened lotus, borne of water, represent its generative power. The god Vishnu in his incarnation as a turtle is represented as the base for the churning of the primordial ocean of milk.

Above left: Nandī, the bull, the vehicle of Shiva, is a common motif and symbol of fertility in Indian art.

Head of Nandī. *19th century. Painted wood, 30⅞ x 15¼" (75 x 42 cm). AIHB Crafts Museum, New Delhi.*

Above right: Papier mâché depiction of Shiva, Pārvatī, and Nandī.

Shiva and Pārvatī with Nandī. *Contemporary. Painted papier mâché, 7 x 5 x 3" (18¼ x 13 x 8 cm). HHEC Collection, New Delhi.*

Above: Women at the holy site of Pushkar, Rajasthan prepare to worship the stone linga and yoni, which represents the god Shiva in whom is combined the creative forces of the universe: male and female.

Mukha linga: The personified image of Shiva as Vira a warrior. This hollow brass image is placed on top of the natural or carved stone lingam at the time of worship.

Mukha Linga. *Mid-18th century. Bronze, 12½ x 5¼" (33 x 13½ cm). Collection of Lance Dane, Bombay.*

Symbols of human fertility are richly drawn from the domains of nature, the gods, animals, and crafted products. Human fertility and desire may be symbolized in animal form, popularly as a snake, the *kundalinī*, which begins to stir at puberty and rises in adolescence. The snake, a particularly potent symbol of fertility and desire, expresses the creative awakening of independent India:

> *When the snake-charmer's hour-glass drum is shaken How can the darkhooded snake stay coiled any longer down its hole?*
> (Michael Madhusudan Datta, poet and playwright of the Bengal resurgence, nineteenth century)[6]

Other animals—the fleet parakeet, the strutting peacock, the stud bull, and the elephant—are also used to convey messages of human love in classical literature and the folk arts.

This lamp, replete with male and female symbolism, is carried by the sister of the bride as she walks behind the couple to their marriage ceremony. The *nāga*, or cobra snake, representing fertility rises above the basin, the female principle, that contains the wick, the phallic form.

Diyā. *18th century. Brass, 9¾ x 7⅛" (25 x 19 cm). Raja Dinkar Kelkar Museum, Pune.*

Ardhanārīshvara: This image of the god Shiva illustrates the dual nature of the godhead where the right half of the image is male—Shiva (to the reader's left)—and the left half is female, the goddess Umā.

Ardhanārīshvara. *20th century. Metal, 20⅞ x 10¾ x 7¾" (70 x 28 x 20 cm). AIHB Regional Design Centre, Bangalore.*

Crafts also provide for rich imagery of fertility. Kilns throughout the country are revered as the womb of the goddess. Temple potters from Orissa believe that the fires which bake their holy pots and hence bring them into existence are empowered by the conjoining fertility of god and goddess. A lamp, with a basin "womb" for cotton seed or other oil and a "phallic" spire wick for burning, unites complementary powers of fertility. Objects used in everyday life—the grinding stone and the churn, the winnowing fan, the plow, and the pounder—also serve as idioms for expressing male and female fertility, as through their use extant matter is transformed into something new.

Above right: A clay toy-maker in Varanasi puts the finishing touches on a toy parakeet. The unrestrained intimacy of parakeets, often seen "kissing" and preening each other on a branch, has resulted in their becoming an important symbol—the messenger of Kāma, the god of love.

Right: A village potter in Bhuj, Gujarat becomes the creator, *prajāpati*, as he forms simple vessels from a lump of clay.

The everyday chore of churning butter from milk has been likened to the creation of the world when the gods and demons churned the primeval ocean of milk.

Above: Four Māldhārī women work together to turn the churn in a large metal vessel.

Left: A painted leather puppet scene depicts two milkmaids, or *gopīs*, of Vrindāvan churning butter beneath a spreading tree.

Leather Puppet of Women Churning. *Contemporary. Painted leather, 20½ x 19″ (61 x 49 cm). Chitrakala Parishad, Bangalore.*

Right: These ancient bronze figures from Chanda, Maharashtra (5th to 6th century A.D.) depict a warrior and his consort. The female figure is holding a mirror and is ornamented with bangles, a necklace, and a girdle.

Erotic Couple. *5th to 6th century. Brass, 3½ x 2⅛" (9 x 5½ cm). Collection of Pupul Jayakar, New Delhi.*

Below: Village women in Rajasthan paint a figure of the goddess on their home to ensure fertility and prosperity.

Opposite top: These small clay figures of Shiva (right) and Pārvatī with child (left) are clothed and decorated for the Gangour Festival in Madhya Pradesh. Women who carry these figures on their head during the festival pray for children and the well-being of their household.

Gangour Figures of Shiva, Pārvatī and Baby. *Contemporary. Terra cotta. Left: 5¾ x 2¼ x 2¼," (15 x 5¾ x 5¾ cm). Right: 6½ × 2½ × 2" (17 × 6⅓ × 5¼ cm). Roopankar, Bharat Bhavan, Bhopal.*

Opposite bottom: Rāj Mandhana, a painting of the Kangra School, shows a maiden embracing a banana tree, invoking the themes of fertility and marriage.

For Indians, the fertility that symbolizes creation and life can also be dangerous if mis-directed. As the child comes of age, a blossoming fertility suggests the potential for union and the recreation of the macrocosmic acts of gods and goddesses, earth and sky. But such a union has to be arrived at properly so that it may be fruitful and auspicious. Girls and boys may be separtated; spurious and impulsive unions are discouraged. Fertility, as the power which creates and sustains the universe, the environment, and the social order, must be handled carefully.

Where shall we begin?
Before the infant even makes its
   appearance,
We have been expecting it, hoping for it,
Invoking its presence among us to gladden
   our lives and extend our community.
When the girl first begins to weep blood
   at the time of the moon's filling,
And when the boy takes on his father's
   trade and learns to be a man,
We know that the flower is beginning to
   open.
Soon, very soon,
We shall prepare for yet another
   generation.

II. Courtship and Betrothal

This Warli painting shows the betrothed couple in a spiraling circle of dancing boys and girls.

Jivya Soma. Warli Pictograph. *Contemporary. Tribal Museum, Pune.*

Overleaf: A tribal youth from Orissa plays the flute as his lover rests beside him. This age-old scene is repeated again and again in the stories of Krishna and the milkmaids.

Although betrothal concerns two individuals, in traditional India it is largely a community affair. Marriages are typically arranged by the parents of a prospective couple. Families may approach each other through the help of relatives, friends, or even professional matchmakers as they seek appropriate lifemates for their children. Betrothal attends to the concerns of caste, community interests, and the advice of astrologers to insure that the match is both socially and cosmologically auspicious.

The selection of a bride for one's son or a bridegroom for one's daughter is made by parents and elders after careful deliberation.

It has been done with honor.
The parents have met and sat gravely
    side by side
Gifts have been exchanged.

It is a good family, honorable,
    known to us.

As depicted in Warli pictographs from Maharashtra, the knot that binds the couple upon betrothal is celebrated by the whole community—for the knot of honor and life-sharing replicated between bride and bridegroom is one that binds together families and society as a whole.

In much of traditional India, the future bride and bridegroom may meet only briefly or even not at all before preparations are underway for the marriage. While courtship is not generally conducted in the contemporary Western sense of "dating," it may nonetheless occur in a more subtle, non-immediate form. Prospective brides and bridegrooms are frequently encouraged to idealize their future relationship. In such musings girls and boys may be encouraged to identify with goddesses and gods or the heroines and heros of folk tales, such as Sītā and Rāma, in an effort to give shape to their roused emotions.

Left: Contemporary carving of a Naga youth. Similar figures were carved on the façade of the *morung*—the tribal dormitory for adolescent boys—to commemorate a boy's coming of age or the taking of enemy heads.

Konyak Naga Figure. *Contemporary. Wood, cloth, and leather, 10¼ x 5½ x 3⅞″ (32 x 15 x 10 cm). AIHB Crafts Museum, New Delhi.*

Below left: A youth's time in the morning was often spent in carving elaborate items such as this tobacco pipe, to attract the attention of marriageable girls.

Tobacco Pipe with Carved Human Figure. *Contemporary. Wood, 5¼ x 2 x 1¼″ (13½ x 5¼ x 3 cm). National Museum, New Delhi.*

Below: In the past, a boy was considered ready for marriage only if he had killed an enemy or helped in taking a head. This wooden knife, carved with the shape of a human head and decorated with horsehair, was worn as a trophy during village dances and courtship.

Ritual Object with Carving of Human Head and Hair. *Contemporary. Wood and hair, 1½ x 9″ (4 x 23½ cm). Collection of Pupul Jayakar, New Delhi.*

What he said:

Does that girl, eyes like flowers,
Gathering flowers from pools for her garlands,
Driving away the parrots from the millet fields—
Does that girl know at all, or doesn't she,
That my heart is still there with her . . ?
(Kapilar, poet of the Chankam period, south
India, A.D. 100-300)[7]

What she said to the messenger:

Tell me,

Did you really see him,
Or did you just hear it from someone who did see
him?
I want to make sure . . .

But tell me first,
From whose mouth did you hear of my lover's
coming?
(Patumarattu Mochikiranar, poet of the
Chankam period, south India, A.D. 100-300)[8]

The communal dormitory, or ghotul of the
Muria tribes of central India is one of several alter-
natives to the Hindu norm. Moving from their
family homes into the communal dormitory of the
village, post-pubescent children will remain there
through their teens, until they are old enough to
set up homes of their own. The ghotul is remarkable for its emphasis on the absence of private
property and the discouragement of possessiveness
in relationships. Its leaders, a boy and a girl, are
elected annually by the children themselves. The
adolescents are initiated into the act of love by
their peers. Their extensive range of courtship
songs is unusual in its tenderness; boys carve
combs for the girls and girls carve tobacco-holders
for the boys to tuck into their turbans or sashes.
Yet the evening rituals of collective massage and of
group dancing discourage any permanent form of
pairing or excessive attachment within the com-
mune. Instead, togetherness—the communal basis
of ghotul life among the Muria—is encouraged.

In the pastoral setting of Vraja, Krishna, the divine lover, entices the milk-maids with his enchanting flute music. Even the animals stop to listen. Call of the Flute. *Mid-19th century. Painting on paper, 10½ x 8¾" (33 x 23 cm). Collection of Amit Ambalal, Ahmedabad.*

55

III. Preparation for
the Wedding

Maithilī artist Sita Devi paints traditional wedding motifs on panels at the Crafts Museum in New Delhi.

Accompanying betrothal, gifts in the form of sweets, clothing, and jewelry pass between the two families. A date for the wedding is arranged with the help of an astrologer. The future bride and bridegroom, curious and apprehensive about married life, are instructed about its pleasures, pains, and mysteries by relatives and friends through song, riddles, and ritual activities.

Wall paintings produced in the Mithilā region of Bihar illustrate both the transmission of such knowledge and the way in which the myths of the gods are called upon to inform human relationships. Girls begin at an early age to draw paintings known as *kohbar*. At the time of her marriage, a kohbar is painted on the walls of her nuptial chamber as a present to her bridegroom. The kohbar is heavily charged with symbolism of male and female, and draws freely upon images of Shiva, Pārvatī, and their offspring Ganesha. Mithilā paintings invoke the presence of the god Krishna playing with the milkmaids, or the story of Rāma and his wife, Sītā, the godly hero and heroine of the Rāmāyana who are often presented as the model for human couples.

As the marriage proper generally occurs at the home of the bride, her family arranges for the marital ritual, the groom's entourage, and the general celebrations, which last for several days. The home of the bride is thoroughly cleaned and purified. Live banana trees, with fruits and flowers, may be planted to flank the gateway. The dowry must be assembled and preparations made for the wedding feasts, to which relatives, friends, neighbors and the groom's people will be invited.

Overleaf:
p. 56: Octagonal papier mâché dowry box with painted panels depicting religious scenes.

Papier Mâché Dowry Box. *Kashmir. Late 19th century. Indian Museum, Calcutta.*

p. 57: Fresco of a bride holding a mirror as she prepares herself for the wedding. Rajasthan.

This Maithilī painting on paper depicts Shiva being fanned by his consort Pār-vatī. Paintings such as these—chosen to provide subtle reminders to the bride and groom of their respective duties—are often executed on the mud walls of the nuptial chamber.

Ritual floor paintings are done by women to welcome gods into the home or the temple.

As the day of the wedding approaches, the gods and goddesses must be summoned to insure an auspicious beginning to the marriage. A slender woman in a white *sari* crouches over the floor. On the gold-brown adobe surface already primed with cowdung, her hand lets fall precisely measured dots of ground white rice powder. These she unhesitantly connects, forming lines and shapes. This is the floor-drawn *mandala*—known as *aripan* in Bihar, *māndnā* in Rajasthan, *rangolī* in Gujarat, *ālpanā* in Bengal, and *kolam* in south India. The maze of lines under her loose fingers emerges to enclose graduated areas of sacral space. The whole is symbolic and auspicious, a channel between humans and gods.

The young girls standing by look on with keen interest. She herself is silent. The mandala completed, she dots the center of geometrical figures with ritual vermillion, hence activating it and invoking the presence and the powers of the gods.

What passes through her mind? Is she looking back to the great day in her own life when she was married? Or has her mind slipped back into stillness? Does she note that she has, with both preoccupation and dignity, transmitted one of the sixty-four classical arts of ancient India and fulfilled at the same time the religious code for householders?

If she is from the Mithilā villages of Bihar, she certainly knows, even if she does not mention it, that she has been entrusted with an art whose guardianship is given to women alone. And she is secure in the fact that her mother made just such a mandala for her, as her daughter will make for her own daughter's marriage when the time comes. She measures it one last time with her eyes before she turns to wash her hands in the courtyard.

She would like to spend a few quiet minutes before the day closes with her daughter, the first to leave home. She will open the container in the double-locked box beneath the bed and parcel out some of the jewelry she received as her own dowry, reserving the rest to share among the younger ones. The saris, the traditional toiletry, and the gleaming household vessels have been packed.

A grandmother lovingly
adorns the bride with jewelry that is an important
part of her dowry.

The occasion of a wedding requires many gifts to be exchanged between the families of the betrothed, and craftsmen are required to produce unique and elaborate items for ritual or daily use.

Above: Brass betel nut holder in the shape of a peacock, which is a symbol of courtship.
Raja Dinkar Kelkar Museum, Pune.

Right: Ornate combs carved from ebony.

*Contemporary. Top: 6"
(16 cm); bottom: 6½"
(18 cm). Collection of Amar
Nath, New Delhi.*

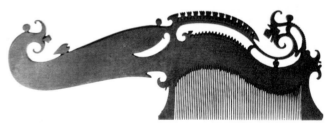

This eldest daughter is shy and inward-looking today, understandably quite unlike her normal self. No other occasion in her life will demand so much of her: the seriousness of the ceremony, the first encounter with her husband, and especially the close scrutiny by her new family. Even when the children come it's easier.

Her anxieties will ease and settle, of course, and the joys will begin. This is the best time. But it is not always easy to be a woman. There can be nothing richer if one is fortunate, and wise. And the girl will be on her own tomorrow in a very real and private sense, for she will have become a woman.

In the inner chamber meanwhile, the
   young girl's senses are shyly coming awake.
Older women have bathed her affection-
   ately in a cleansing golden wash of tum-
   eric water or sandal paste.
Her startled eyes are lined with *kājal*
   made from the soot of tender nim flowers.

Her slender palms and the soles of her
   feet, heated with expectancy, are dyed
   to an intricate tracery of copper-colored
   leaves and tendrils with the cool juice of
   crushed henna.

And her hair, washed with three fruits,
   has been dried over incense, oiled and coiled.
Fresh flower-chains are being carried in
   by the basket;
Jasmine, rose and the bittersweet fire of marigold;
Their scent lands in the air.
The bed is disordered with silks; each a
   classic, as far as possible, of its tradition.
For this is her inheritance.
Boxes of ancestral jewels are being uncovered.
These she receives from her mother and
   from her grandmother.
These she will wear for the first time tonight;
And these tomorrow take away for daughters
   of her own.

Elaborate brass cosmetic holder from south India in the form of a woman holding a mirror in her right hand and a container for vermillion or eyeliner in her left. She is standing on a turtle, an auspicious symbol, representing the foundation on which the universe rests.

Woman Standing on a Tortoise. *Early 19th century. Brass, 4 x 2½ x 2¼" (10½ x 6½ x 6 cm). National Museum, New Delhi.*

Female relatives of the
bride prepare her for the
wedding by applying
mehndī to her hands and
feet.

Preparations for the bride include bodily adornment and songs teasing her about relatives in the household of her husband-to-be. *Benares Hindu University, Bharat Kala Bhavan.*

Both the bride and the bridegroom must be prepared for the marriage. Widespread among Hindus is the belief that a wife becomes the "half-body" of her husband, linked to him physically, socially, and morally. Marriage, for a girl, is a second birth, for in the patrilineal communities of India, she is known by her husband's name, joins his clan, and lives with his family. Marital preparations symbolize this new state by transforming the appearance, primarily of the bride, but also of the groom. This is done through ritual baths, changing of clothes, and bodily adornment.

The application of *mehndī*, or henna, which prepares the couple for marriage, is common among both Hindus and Muslims of north India. Before the wedding intricate designs are painted on the hands of the bride and bridegroom. The henna is said to have a cooling and beautifying effect, bringing to the surface, yet containing the sensuality and creative power of the prospective couple.

> *The henna has sprouted a pair of leaves,*
> *The love juice of henna is a lovely tint. . .*
> *Oh lady, who has painted your hands?*
> *The live juice of henna is a lovely tint. . .*
> *Oh lady, put your hands on my heart,*
> *The love juice of henna is a lovely tint. . .*
> (Mehndī song of Mewār)[9]

While some groups prefer the pale golden latticework of languid arabesques, the desert dwellers of Rajasthan extract a blood red dye of which they say, "The deeper the red of the henna, the deeper the love between husband and wife."[10]

Brass hairpiece in the form of a female acrobat with a pair of parrots—a symbol of courtship. Ornaments such as this are included in a bride's trousseau.

Hair Dryer in Shape of Female. *18th century. Brass, 8 x 2¾ x 1¼" (21 x 7¼ x 3½ cm). Government Museum, Madras.*

IV. The Wedding Procession

The bridegroom prince has arrived at the border of
  the village;
He is trembling oh king (of love).
The bridegroom prince has arrived at the garden;
He is trembling oh king (of love).
The bridegroom prince has arrived at the bridal
  gateway;
He is trembling oh king (of love).
The bridegroom prince has arrived at the place of
  the seven wedding paces;
He is trembling oh king (of love).
(*Barāt* or wedding procession song, from
  Mewār)[11]

Weddings in India typically occur over several
days and include many activities and celebrations
in addition to the actual marriage ceremony. The
bridegroom's procession is a dramatic prelude to
the traditional north Indian marriage. Announced
by lights, fireworks, singing, drums and horns, the
triumphal bridegroom rides resplendent in the glit-
ter of ceremonial costume atop a mare, elephant, or
camel and backed by an escort of companions and
relatives, sets out toward the bride's home.

Overleaf: Royal procession showing a prince on a caparisoned horse. The bridegroom is dressed in a similar manner when led to claim his bride.

B.G. Sharma. Wall Painting. *Contemporary.*

The sister of this Bakar-wala nomad of Kashmir decorates his eyes with kājal to accentuate their beauty. A garland of rupee notes provides for an auspicious beginning to his married life.

A bridegroom on the way
to his wedding in Bombay.

Crowds collect and children watch with eyes of wonder. The spirit of the event is captured by the *kacchī ghorī*, or "play horse" dance of Rajasthan, in which the excitement of the procession, the sensuality of the marital relationship, and the dominance of the bridegroom and his relatives are joyously expressed.

The approach of the procession announces the upcoming union in all the villages and neighborhoods it passes. The music of the procession is jarringly loud, and purposefully so, signifying to all that it is with honor and without deceit that this groom is on his way to claim his bride.

The arrival of the procession is awaited with anticipation by the bride's family and well-wishers. As the procession enters her village, its members may be offered sweets or refreshing drinks by residents in an open display of hospitality.

At the bride's house, the mounted bridegroom advances to claim his bride. With a crown of flowers and sword in hand, he touches the *toran* or gatepost ornament before being greeted with auspicious colors, food, and by the bride's mother and female relatives who apply the *tīkā* (forehead dot). Among Muslims, the relatives and friends of both bride and groom form reception lines and those of the groom's procession are greeted, hugged, and given garlands.

Opposite: Wedding gifts are displayed for all to see the generosity of the new relatives.

Above: Kacchī ghorī or play-horse dancers mimic the pageantry of the wedding procession with drums and a make-believe mare.

71

V. The Wedding

Let there be no quarrels.
Let there be many children.
As the root is below,
And the branches above,
So may we be united.
(Muria tribal marriage song, from central India)[12]

Weddings in India bring into focus much about the country's culture and social life. *Vivāha*, the formal Hindu marriage, is at once an individual rite of passage, a religious sacrament, and a socio-economic transaction between families and clans.

The wedding accomplishes the marriage of two families by joining together of bride and bridegroom. For this purpose, the groom and bride are enshrined as a godly king and queen. Attired magnificently and wearing ritual crowns, they may be seated on symbolic thrones to be viewed and, in a sense, worshipped. For they, as a pair to be joined, represent and encapsulate the creative activity which spawned the universe.

I am the man, you the woman.
I the chant, you the word.
I am the sky, you the earth.
Come, let us be together.
From us let children spring.
(Wedding response of traditional Hindu marriage, Atharva Veda 4:2:71, 1200-900 B.C.)[13]

Above: A Sikh wedding is held in the presence of the Granth Sāhib, the holy scriptures. These scriptures are set on an elaborate lectern and draped with brocade, which will be removed when the officiating priest begins the ceremony.

Opposite top: A tribal wedding in Arunachal Pradesh.

Overleaf:

p. 72: A vegetable knife in the form of a parrot, the symbol of love and courtship, is often included in the dowry of a bride.

Vegetable Cutter. *Late 19th century. Iron, 14 x 13½″ (36½ x 35 cm). Raja Dinkar Kelkar Museum, Pune.*

p. 73: Krishna's wedding to Rukminī. The bride and groom perform the ritual oblations to the sacred fire, Agni, as Brāhman priests recite the scriptures. The four-cornered pavilion draped with auspicious mango leaves represents the four corners of the world. *Benares Hindu University, Bharat Kala Bhavan.*

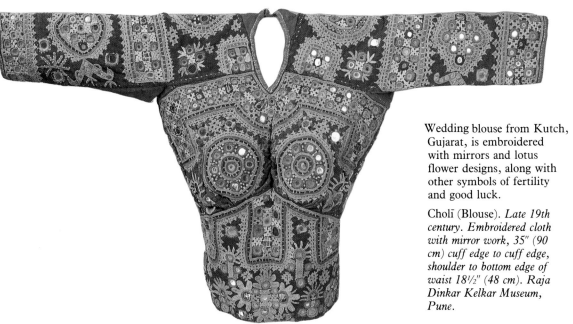

Wedding blouse from Kutch, Gujarat, is embroidered with mirrors and lotus flower designs, along with other symbols of fertility and good luck.

Cholī (Blouse). *Late 19th century. Embroidered cloth with mirror work, 35" (90 cm) cuff edge to cuff edge, shoulder to bottom edge of waist 18¹/₂" (48 cm). Raja Dinkar Kelkar Museum, Pune.*

Dowry items, given by the bride's family for her to take to her new home, are often displayed and commented upon for their lavishness, or lack thereof. Dowry represents a woman's movable property in those parts of the country where land and homestead are inherited from father to son. A woman's dowry typically includes her trousseau, cooking vessels and implements ranging from brass to silver, the jewelry she inherits from her mother, home-crafted items she has learned to make, and most personally her cosmetic chest.

Some of these items will enrich the communal homestead of her husband's family. Some will be used for her own needs and those of her husband. Her jewelry is highly valued, not only because it represents the finest of local craft traditions and may have been especially commissioned for the event, but also because it can be easily converted to cash in times of need.

Opposite: The two domed containers, *sindūr dān*, are a part of the bride's dowry. They hold the sacred vermillion or *sindūr* that is put in the part of her hair and on her forehead as a symbol of marriage. The flat container would hold *pān* and betel nut or tobacco to be served to the husband and guests.

Containers. *Late 19th century. Painted wood, (left) 8¼ x 9¾" (21 x 25 cm); (center) 5¾ x 6" (15 x 15½ cm); (right) 2 x 8" (5 x 21 cm). AIHB Crafts Museum, New Delhi.*

Above left: The damascened gold designs of flowers and vines on this regal water pot are symbols of health and prosperity.

Iron Lotā Inlaid with Gold. *Late 19th century. Damascene technique, 8 x 6" (21 x 15¾ cm). Indian Museum, Calcutta.*

Glazed ceramic jar decorated with auspicious peacocks. Similar jars filled with nuts or dried fruits are often included among the wedding gifts.

Ceramic Jar with Peacock Motif. *Late 19th century. Terra cotta, 12¾ x 9" (33 x 24 cm). Indian Museum, Calcutta.*

Right: Elaborately painted tray for serving *pān-supārī* at the wedding or other festive occasions. The auspicious flowers, parakeets, and ground squirrels ensure good luck and prosperity.

Tray with Floral Design (on Four Legs). *Late 19th century. Papier mâché, 15¼ x 2″ (40 x 5¼ cm). Indian Museum, Calcutta.*

Below: A tray of sweets from a confectionary in Varanasi is displayed at the wedding. Sweets made from milk, sugar, and nuts are topped with edible pure silver and gold foil.

Opposite: A woman is shown preparing food in the courtyard of a palace, while a boy looks on. The girl in the foreground is using a vegetable cutter similar to the one depicted earlier (page 72).

Painting. *Kangra School. 1780. Central Museum, Lahore, Pakistan.*

For the bride's family, providing a feast for the wedding guests is a matter of honor, and the choice of food—rich with clarified butter, rice with saffron, and delectable sweets—reflects upon the family's economic and social position. North Indian weddings may come alive with song and dance to entertain assembled guests. Itinerant performers, slapstick artists, and comedians may turn up at the marriage celebration. And special dances such as the *saperā*, or snake dance, of the Nats of Rajasthan may be performed especially for the occasion.

Although sometimes performed in temples, particularly in south India, the Hindu marriage ceremony more usually occurs in a specially consecrated area of the bride's household courtyard. There, under a canopy, the sacred fire, regarded as a receiver of offerings and conduit to the gods, is attended by a Brāhman priest. Under his guidance, the bride and groom are instructed to recite various ancient verses, and to feed the fire with clarified

butter, seeds, and grain. The ritual joining of bride and groom reaches its climax with the seven circumambulations of the sacred fire. With the garment of the bride tied to that of the groom, she is led around the fire. In the folk culture of patrilineal communities of Hindu India, this is perceived as a tightening of her bonds to her husband and his family and a concommitant unwinding or dissolution of her ties to her own family.

> *Here she makes the first circle, her grandfather's*
> *granddaughter.*
> *Here she makes the second circle, her mother's*
> *brother's maternal niece.*
> *Here she makes the third circle, her father's elder*
> *brother's niece.*
> *Here she makes the fourth circle, her father's own*
> *daughter.*
> *Here she makes the fifth circle, her father's younger*
> *brother's niece.*
> *Here she makes the sixth circle, her brother's sister.*
> *Here she makes the seventh circle, and lo!, the*
> *darling becomes alien to our family.*
> (A marriage song from a north Indian village)[14]

The beginning of one way of life, and the end of another are represented once again by the circle.

The break need not always be so radical. She will visit her family at least once a year, often on a particular festival. And she is likely to return home to bear her first child. But it is the idea of *kanyā dān*, the giving away of a daughter, that accounts for much of the underlying poignancy of the event, including the feasting and the giving of other gifts to the groom's family.

Opposite:
The bride and groom must
perform many rituals in the
course of the marriage ceremony which generally
lasts for several days,
depending on the families'
means.

Rosewater sprinkler in the
shape of a fish, a symbol of
fertility and good luck.
Such sprinklers are used to
anoint the wedding guests
and the wedding food with
sweet-smelling rosewater.

Rosewater Sprinkler. *Contemporary. Brass, 10" (26
cm). AIHB Crafts Museum,
New Delhi.*

Above: Hollow brass coco-
nuts filled with stones are
used in the Natangu wed-
ding ceremony in Tamil
Nadu. The bride and
groom roll the coconut rattles back and forth. The
coconut is an auspicious
fruit because it yields oil,
pure sweet water, and
nutritious pulp.

Hollow Replica of Coconut.
*Contemporary. Brass.
HHEC and the collection of
O.P. Jain, New Delhi.*

This painted wooden box
is used to carry various
dowry items to the new
home of the bride. One
panel depicts the devī, the
mother goddess, in her
symbolic form: a pottery
vessel filled with water and
covered by mango leaves
and a coconut. Two fish,
symbols of fertility and
good luck, are shown on
either side.

Dowry Box. *Contemporary.
Wood with starched and
painted cloth, 13 x 13 x
20⅛" (34 x 34 x 54 cm).
AIHB Crafts Museum, New
Delhi.*

Much uneasy playfulness attends an Indian wedding. In many regions, bride and groom may be seated together, perhaps for the first time, and in front of close relatives asked to greet each other. A veil may be lifted. Each might gaze at the reflection of the other in a mirror or a pan of water. And the groom might ask his bride to verbally acknowledge his authority. For his turn, the groom may be subjected to various trials. Sisters of the bride may refuse to admit him to the house until he pays them a ritual bribe. The groom, perhaps accompanied by one or two close friends, may be questioned by an assembly of the bride's female relatives and friends. He may have to answer difficult riddles, or be asked to climb a greased pole. Younger, mischievous relatives of the bride may sneak off with his shoes and challenge him to find them. All of this is quite ritualized and, while done in fun, it also allows friends and relatives to assess the physical and psychological compatability of bride and groom.

The many variations in marriage customs in India include the norms of the Sanskritic and Dravidian classical traditions, the influence of Hindu, Muslim, Christian, Sikh, Buddhist, Jewish, Jain, and Zoroastrian ideas, and the practices of diverse tribal, peasant, and urban communities.

Among the Nayar community of Kerala, land and property were inherited matrilineally. The bonds between mothers and their children, and between brothers and sisters were highly valued. The strength of the clan through the bloodline was more important than the incorporation of outsiders through marriage. Marriage itself was a solemn contract between man and woman, although among the Nayar, a woman might legitimately have more than one lover to father her children. Even today, Nayar weddings are simple in comparison to those of more mainstream Hindu communities. Clad in white and gold, surrounded by flowering coconut, and positioned in front of a standing lamp, the couple formally exchanges gifts of wearing apparel and are blessed by family elders.

There are many other regional, religious, and ethnic variations. For Sikhs of the Punjab, bride and groom together circumambulate the Adi Granth, their holy book. For Muslims, the central act of marriage is the joint affirmation of the *nikāh-nāma*, or wedding contract. For all communities, however, there is the recognition of a ritual joining, a tying together of the bridegroom and bride as a physical, social, and moral unity.

Ceremony, feasting, and entertainment completed, the bride and groom begin their life together. In northern India, the separation of the newly wed bride from her family is marked by her departure from their house and her travel with the groom's procession back to his town or village. Before leaving she may be blessed by her parents, given a last drink of milk, or, as in the case of Muslims, exit the house under the shadow of the Quran. Traditionally carried in a palanquin, the bride is accompanied by an elder kinswoman or in some cases, a midwife who will instruct and help her prepare for the nuptial night.

Right: This ritual oil lamp with dangling rattles and symbols of fertility—the square knots and the shoots of grass—is carried by the bride's mother as she welcomes the bridegroom. After the wedding it is given to the bride to take to her new home.

Diyā. *Late 19th century. Iron, 25½ x 19¼" (61 x 50 cm). Raja Dinkar Kelkar Museum, Pune.*

Opposite top: In a Hindu wedding the bride and groom, symbolically joined with a scarf, must circle the sacred fire before the ceremony is complete.

Left: The bride's family, friends, and neighbors look on as she departs for the groom's village, in this glimpse of life among the Bakarwala nomads of Jammu and Kashmir.

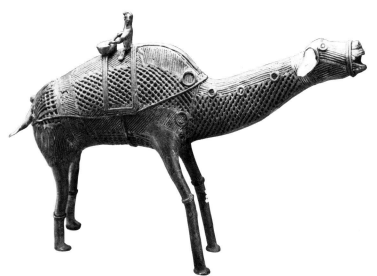

Left: The groom and his friends and relatives lead the bride away to her new home. Her face and body are covered to protect her from the stares of strangers.

Above: Votive image of a drummer or herald seated on a camel. Such items are given to the bride as wedding souvenirs.

Drummer Seated on a Camel. *Contemporary. Brass, 7 x 9¾" (18 x 25 cm) nose to tail. Government Museum, Madras.*

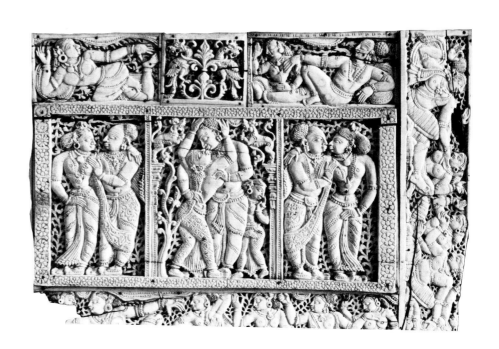

VI. The Wedding Night

On the wedding night, an effort is made by the groom's family to provide the newly married couple with sights, tastes, scents, and sensations indicative of their special relationship.

The nuptial chamber of a *nawāb*, a Muslim lord of the gentry, from nineteenth century Lucknow, reflects this to the extreme. Recalling the imperial luxury of former Mughal glory, the room is made to order for the nuptial night. It is in this room that the newly married couple first face each other alone, and the first time that they can begin to show affection for one another. A sense of leisure and fantasy is deliberately invoked in the chamber.

The arches of the chamber are elaborately fluted and the niches stylized. The sky is symbolized by the ceiling awning, and the naturalness of the occasion suggested by fresh, scented flowers. Bands around the bed legs keep the bed clothes in place. Not a single crease will irritate the occupants. The seating area is of plush velour. Bolsters and soft pillows can be arranged to suit every posture. Red, the bridal color, considered auspicious, is repeated in many hues. Brocades are the preferred textile, and raised embroidery in gold and silver threads the favored draping. Appliqué colored silks in geometric designs form the covers for the Quran and for the cask of aromatics used in making *pān*—a mildly stimulating condiment.

Everything that the couple needs is here. There are silver tumblers and bowls, a silver flask, a long-stemmed sprinkler for rose water, and a delicate perfume container. The bride's elaborate toiletries are at hand around her cosmetic chest. The groom's *hukkā* awaits him, its tobacco bowl replete with ornate relief work, silver chains adorning its cover, and detachable mouthpieces for its winding stem. On this occasion, no ordinary tobacco is smoked in this water pipe. Syrup, spices, and perfumes will transform tobacco fumes into incense. The serving and chewing of pan leaf and betal nut is an essential part of this culture. The cask and server are necessities, the spittoon an essential convenience. There is a ewer and a basin with an intricately perforated cover to hide the used water. Fresh grass is spread over this cover so that the water does not splash when poured.

Overleaf:
p. 84: Carved panels of an ivory box depict the royal couple in their nuptial chamber attended by male and female servants. This jewelry box was also part of the bedroom furniture of King Thirumalai Nāyaka.

Carved Ivory Box. *17th century. Ivory, 13 x 13" (34 x 34 cm). Sri Ranganthaswami Devasthanas Museum.*

p. 85: Carved and painted ivory figures of amorous couples, or *mithuna*. These figures were used to decorate the bedchamber of King Thirumalai Nāyaka, who ruled from Thanjavur in the 17th century.

Amorous Couples. *17th century. Ivory, 11 x 12" (29 x 31 cm). Sri Ranganathaswami Devasthanas Museum, Tamil Nadu.*

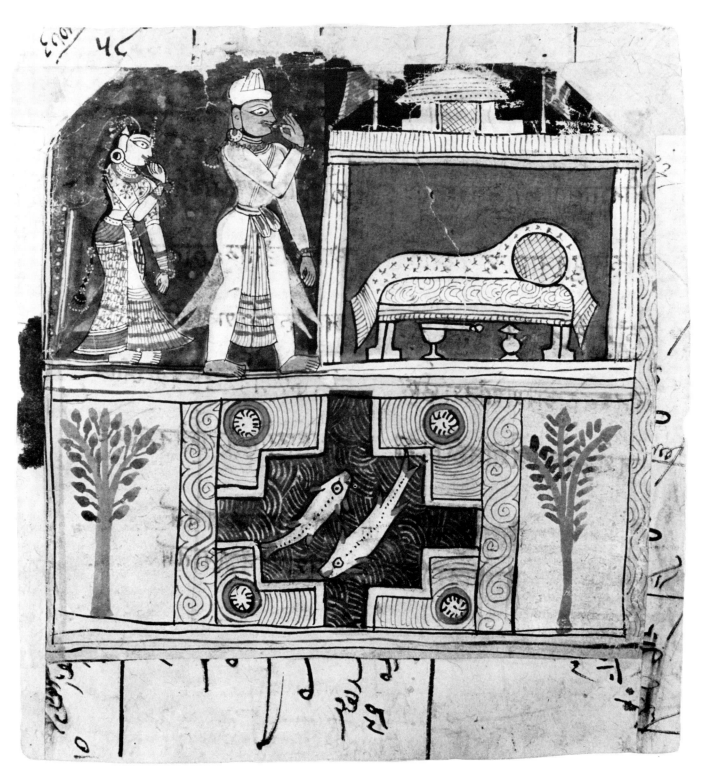

An illustration from the
Mrigāvat shows a man
leading a woman to a bed-
chamber. Two fish, an auspicious symbol of fertility,
are seen swimming in the
courtyard pool, which is
bordered by two growing
trees.

Painting Depicting Scene
from *Mrigāvat. 1520. Early
Rajasthan. Paper gouache,
7¼ x 6¾" (19 x 18 cm).
Varanasi.*

Top: Traditional games such as *chausar* or *pachīsī* often help the newly-weds to become more acquainted. *Raja Dinkar Kelkar Museum, Pune.*

Above: Erotic scenes decorate these rolling lamps that provide suggestive movements as the light flickers in the fretwork.

Khel Diyā (Rolling Lamps). *Mid-18th century. Brass, 5½" dia. (14 cm). Raja Dinkar Kelkar Museum, Pune.*

There are reminders in this room of the marriage rituals. The Quran is there, high in the background on a lecturn. Excerpts from the Quran sanctify the Muslim marriage, and it was under the holy Quran held aloft that the bride left her family and entered her husband's home. There are other symbols too. The fish, a symbol of good luck and fertility, is displayed on the silver urn. The urn contains yoghurt, which will be served with fish. The ewer and basin present could have been used for washing the bride's feet, probably with milk, before she stepped into her husband's house.

Ritual elaboration gives culture its glamour, and fundamental institutions and events, such as marriage and the wedding night are rightful subjects for such elaboration. Yet in the privacy of the nuptial chamber, the rules of ritual are modified and elaborated in deeply personal ways. The process of initiation into each other's being takes on private intonations for the newly wed husband and wife.

Even in the simplest of rural homes, in one-room huts made with layers of mud and straw, an effort is made by the groom's family to create a nuptial chamber. Fresh mango leaves, a mirror and an appliqué toran—perhaps embroidered by the bride herself—or an auspicious floor design may mark the entry. An embroidered spread covers the bed, and vermillion, the color of marriage, will somewhere find a place.

Accessories are simple, yet they signal the cooling of passions aroused during the night. There is a shining vessel of a cool drink, a container of aromatic pan and betel leaves, the scent of incense, and the vision of flowers and wedding garlands.

Above: A beaded toran or hanging is made for auspicious occasions such as the wedding night. On the left, the bride and groom are shown in the nuptial bed. On the right, the bride and groom in the wedding ceremony are joined with a garland around their necks.

Toran. *Late 19th and early 20th century. Cloth with seed beads, 10 x 5½" (26 x 14 cm). Raja Dinkar Kelkar Museum, Pune.*

Oh mother, mother,
Half the courtyard has sandalwood trees,
And half the courtyard holds the bridegroom's bed.

The bride says, "A thief has stolen the string of bells
from my cot.
Oh brother, tell me brother,
Who's the thief?"
"Oh sister, little sister
Do not weep.
The thief of the night is
My new brother-in-law."
(Traditional *jog*, a marriage song of union from
Bhojpur.)[15]

Top:
Elaborate betel (areca) nut
cutters in the form of erotic
couples or *mithuna*. Left:
silver, mithuna; center:
brass, Krishna with a gopī;
right: brass, mithuna in
typical Marathi dress of the
mid-19th century.

Betel Nut Cutters. *Mid-*
19th century. Two brass, one
silver. Left: 5¼ x 4" (14 x
10½ cm); center: 6¾ x 3¼"
(17½ x 8 cm); right: 5¼ x
2⅜" (14 x 5½ cm). Raja
Dinkar Kelkar Museum,
Pune.

The Bride:

It is prepared.
They are laughing outside the window—
His friends, his family, those with whom
   he grew up.
Now the doors are closed.
Here is the scent of sandal and of flowers.
There the gods;
And here the scarlet bedspread.
The oil lamp is troubled.
When I looked up from the marriage fire,
I saw him watching me and smiling.
And I changed.
And now?

The Groom:

Tender as the sapling that I planted in my
   father's garden three months ago,
This girl, my wife.
At last we are together.
The pollen has scattered from the flowers
   in her hair,
And she is shy and hesitating by the lamp.
Ah, I will raise for you strong sons and
   daughters, straight of limb and laughing
   proudly.
Come my little bride, my wife.

Top:
The Kāma-sūtra, the ancient
manual for the art of lovemaking, provides numerous
descriptions and illustrations
such as this palm leaf
manuscript from Orissa.
As part of her dowry, it is
often presented to the bride
for her education.
*Institute of Indology,
Ahmedabad*

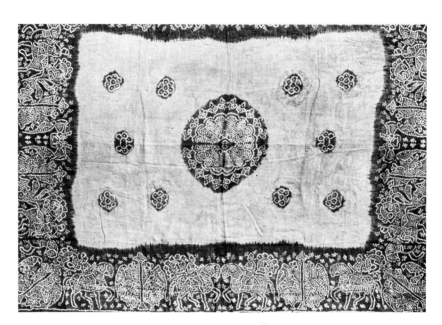

VII. Conception

From dust, then a drop of seed. . . .
(Quran Sharif 22:5)[16]

The act of coupling to bear children is considered a major sacrament in the ancient codes for Hindu householders. The relationship between male and female reproductive roles are often linked to that between seed and field. According to Indian folk biology, male and female reproductive fluids are distillates or concentrations of blood and hence of the bodies of those who produce them. Male fluid, like the seed, is more formative, while female fluid, like the field, is more nurturing. Seeding the field is an act of transferring the power of life, and while to some extent considered a sacrifice, is nonetheless necessary for its perpetuation. When the life-empowering fluids of male and female meet, and if the gods sanction it, a child is conceived. This conception is taken as a sign that indeed the bride and groom, now husband and wife, were and are compatible, justifying the wisdom of the two families. For the husband, conception means his life and his name will continue. For the wife, expectant motherhood solidifies her standing in her husband's family home and indicates that her transformation to one of their own has been accomplished.

In western Rajasthan, the *pīdo*, a turmeric-colored veil with a tie-dyed red dot at its center, is traditionally worn by women who have recently borne a son. Making or asking for the *pīdo* is a way for a wife to communicate her pregnancy and her hope for the birth of a son to her husband.

Overleaf: Pīdo head veil made for an expectant mother. The ten red lotus flowers evoke the months of pregnancy and birth, the central red medallion is the beginning of new life, and the yellow background is the earth. Around the border are parakeets, peacocks, and the bridegroom on horseback.

The wife breaks the news to her husband:

Dear one, the time has come for you to bring me pīdos
The veils my little and elder sisters-in-law already wear.
Your beloved who was envious is now happy.
So glad am I, bring me not one pīdo, but six.
Joyfully drape the first one over my mother-in-law
For she gave life to you.
The second give to my sister-in-law
Who held you in her lap as a child.
The third give to my sister-in-law
Who gave us for a night our very first room of love
Where we played together, turning like the swastika; the travelling sun.
The fourth to my little sister-in-law,
Who gave us the couch on which we rested that same night.
The fifth to the midwife
Who gives me courage to withstand the hour of labor.
And with this sixth pīdo, my husband,
Drape your tender wife who gives you now continuance of your family name.
(Traditional *pīdo* song of Rajasthan)[17]

Opposite: Painted doll portrays a happy mother with auspicious lotus flowers painted on cheeks and chin.

Doll. Contemporary. Painted wood, 6 x 3" (15 x 8 cm). AIHB Crafts Museum, New Delhi.

Above: Village women in Rajasthan wearing pīdo head veils.

VIII. Pregnancy

From the moment of conception, the child is thought to be alive in the womb and susceptible to influence from the world around him. The foods his mother eats, the work she does, the scents she smells, and the words and sounds she hears may all have an effect.

In her husband's house, the other women will help to relieve her of her heavier duties. She will be given good things to eat—items which make her and her child strong and impart desired qualities of temperament. She will be teased and indulged.

As the pregnancy progresses, particularly with a first born, the husband will take his wife back to her childhood home, where she can be comfortable and peaceful and have her own mother to attend to her. Here she will be made much of and spoiled, for she will soon have to return to her duties in her husband's house. For this time, she can be the girl she once was—with the added dignity of a new state. Her childhood friends will visit her, offering food and gifts. And together they will sing songs about the upcoming birth.

> *In the first month, sisters, I desire sweet butter.*
> *In the second month, sweeter coconut molasses.*
> *In the third month, I'm ready for pungent radish.*
> *In the fourth month, sweet balls of lentil ground*
>   *with clarified butter.*
> *In the fifth month, nothing but* makhani *stones.*
> *In the sixth month, coal to stoke the inner fires.*
> *In the seventh month, fresh fried hot and savory*
>   *filled biscuits.*
> *So too in the eight month, simple boiled rice and*
>   *lentils.*
> *But in the ninth month,*
> *Oh by the ninth month sisters,*
> *It's then I wish for halvah, rich and succulent!*
> (*Dohad,* traditional song celebrating
> a pregnant woman's fancies; central
> and northwestern India)[18]

Most of the rituals of pregnancy usually begin in the fifth or seventh month after conception. In Bengal, the seventh-month rite entails an elaborate feast during which gifts are given to the expectant mother. In Tamil Nadu, this event is preceded by her being adorned with bangles and blessed by older women. The bangles symbolize an enclosed circle of protection, containing the creative power within her. The first bangle given is a loop of *nīm* fiber, well known for its therapeutic and healing properties. This is followed by a bangle of elephant hair to impart stamina. A glass bangle conveys the fragility and gaiety of the mother-to-be. Older women, knowledgeable about birth, also offer her quick-sprouting grasses to ease delivery, rice for prosperity, and molasses to sweeten the pain. They may press and massage her back, using a strengthening mixture of rice, turmeric, clarified butter, and milk.

> *While I was in the womb*
> *I knew all the births of the gods.*
> *One hundred steel strongholds guarded me.*
> *I burst out of it*
> *With the swiftness of a hawk.*
> (Aitareya Upanishad 2:1:5, 900-700 B.C.)[19]

Overleaf: A bangle seller at a country fair in Rajasthan displays green glass bangles that are often worn by pregnant women.

Above left: Wooden figure of a female spirit that protects against evil influences and ensures good health.

Female Fetish Figure. *Contemporary. Wood, 16¼ x 2¼" (42 x 6 cm). Government Museum, Madras.*

Opposite: Tribal groups in north India have conceived this drum in the form of a woman, with the womb represented as the drum head.

Musical Instrument. *Contemporary. Wood and parchment, 4¼ x 12⅛" (11 x 32 cm). AIHB Crafts Museum, New Delhi.*

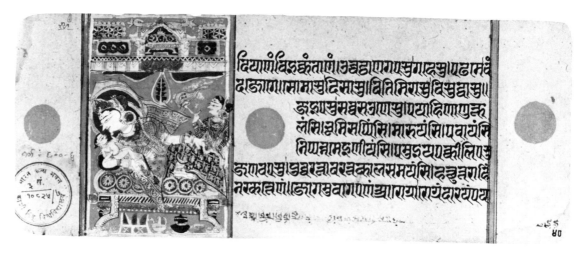

IX. Birth

And being born
I drew in the common air . . .
And the first voice which I uttered
   was crying,
As all others do.
For all men have
One entrance into life,
And the like going out.
(The Holy Bible, Book of Wisdom 7:3,6)[20]

The desert sands of Rajasthan shimmer in the white light of the sun. Shade is prized, water precious. The Rajasthanis, a proud and chivalric people, wear splendid colors. Their joy in living and their musical and artistic traditions seem inexhaustible, perhaps because knowing how hard life can be, they honor and value it more highly.

The time we have been waiting for has
   come.
A great wind sweeps through the old trees
   of the village, bending them and shak-
   ing their fruit.
One of the households has called the
   midwife.
We sit in the courtyard smoking the
   hookah, barely talking.
It is the woman's time.
And now the house belongs to the women,
Busy whispering, heating water, warming
   oil.
The new father starts nervously as a horse
   at each fresh sound from the house.
And we joke with him.
Yes, life is in the balance, but we have
   been through it all before.

And now he is one of us.
For the mother-in-law appears and she is
   smiling.
And the first high cries continue like a
   new bird chirping.
The first lamp is lit.
There is laughing and congratulation.
Quickly announce it with music to the
   village.
And invite the neighbors.
Take out the big family cooking vessels.
In the morning the women will cook with
   clarified butter and sugar and there will
   be sweets for all the neighbors.

Symbolic vessel inscribed with Quranic verses is used to hold water that is drunk by women in labor. Not only does this sanctified water induce and ease labor, but in this manner the word of God is carried to the unborn child.

Symbolic Vessel. *19th century. Brass, 5½ x 1½" (14½ x 4 cm). The Handicrafts and Handlooms Export Corporation of India, Ltd. (HHEC), New Delhi.*

Overleaf: Illustrated text from the *Kalpa-sūtra* depicting the birth of Tīrthankara Mahāvīra, the last of 24 Jain saviors.

Illustrated leaf from the "Kalpa-sūtra." *Late 15th century. Paint on paper, 3¾ x 3¼" (11 x 8 cm). Benares Hindu University, Bharat Kala Bhavan.*

Above: Containers for oil and a lamp that shows their usage. Such lamps are lit during celebrations, including the birth of a baby. Collection of O.P. Jain, New Delhi.

Left: A ritual lamp stand used in the Dīwālī festival combines the auspicious figure of Krishna (top) playing his flute, with a mother and child. Roopankar, Bharat Bhavan, Bhopal.

Contemporary painted wood figure of the baby Krishna with his foster mother Yashodā.

Mother and Child "Yashodā and Krishna." *Contemporary. Painted wood, 9 x 6⅛" (23 x 16 cm). Chitrakala Parishad, Bangalore.*

There is a saying among western Rajasthani women that a woman looks most youthful and desirable when she is drenched in summer rain and when she is gladdened and recovered from childbirth.

The mother's labor is made easier by her mother, the older women of her household, and the ministrations of a midwife experienced in the ancient and traditional arts of childbirth. Pure white desert sand forms the bed for the mother's labor, suitable by virtue of the ease with which it conforms to the woman's shape, its insulating quality, and the fact that it is easily disposed of. As soon as the mother is fully recovered, the baby is carried by a procession of singing women to the nearest well to honor water in the uniquely Rajasthani ceremony of *jalva pūjan*.

As is widespread in northern India, the newborn infant is fed the *gutkī*, or first swallowing. A mixture of honey and clarified butter or sugarcane molasses is first touched to the lips of a relative respected for his or her exemplary qualities, and then touched to the lips of the newborn. The birth is announced by the blowing of conches or the clashing together of metal dishes, if it is a son, or by the clattering of winnowing fans if it is a daughter. The moment of birth is noted, for a horoscope will be cast. The event will occasion a feast for family, relatives, friends, and neighbors. Depending upon the customs of a particular community, naming may occur on the eleventh day after birth, or as late as the hundred-and-first day.

Opposite bottom: This terra cotta image of the protective goddess Shashtī suckling a child is from Assam.

Shashtī and Child. *Contemporary. Terra cotta. 6³⁄₄ x 2²⁄₃ x 1²⁄₃" (17¹⁄₂ x 7 x 4¹⁄₂ cm). Asutosh Museum of Indian Art, Calcutta.*

Above: Sadyojāta—Mother and Child After the Moment of Birth. *Bihar. 8th to 9th century (Pala Dynasty). Stone, 27 x 11¹⁄₂" (71 x 30 cm). Asutosh Museum of Indian Art, Calcutta.*

Painted wooden dolls of mother and child.

Toys—Woman and Child. *19th century. Painted wood, 5¼ and 7⅝" (14 and 20 cm). AIHB Crafts Museum, New Delhi.*

Among the Rajasthanis, the fifteenth day marks the rite of passage known in Sanskrit as the "first outing" but locally known as the "reverence for the sun." The child is ornamented and fully dressed. An area of the courtyard is ritually cleansed and marked with the auspicious sign of the travelling sun. Holding the baby in his arms, the father points to the sun and recites the specified verse from the ancient Sanskrit. If the new father is a man of means, he will feed the brahmin priests in order to have the child blessed through the recitation of auspicious verses.

In these ways, the new life is connected to the old. The infant is introduced into the natural, human, and godly community under the guidance of his or her parents and elders.

From where the sounds of happiness?
Oh friend, from some happy mother's place!
Metal dishes clanged from midnight on with songs of
*   happiness from the father's mother's house!*
And drumming at the mother's mother's house!
At one house greetings,
At the other a darling has just been born.
A moon has risen in a happy mother's courtyard,
Who will rise to take a place of honor
Go tell the sister-in-law to make an offering of
*   lamps!*
(*Halre* or *sohar*, the traditional birth song of northwest India sung by women on the first and sixth day after the birth of a boy)[21]

Above: In Gujarat, a mother and daughter watch over the newborn as it sleeps in a gently swinging hammock.

Left: Both of these dolls from Andhra Pradesh portray a mother and child playing.

Mother and Child. *Contemporary. Modeled wood pulp painted. 5¾ x 4¼" (15 x 11 cm). AIHB Crafts Museum, New Delhi.*

X. Welcoming the Child

The days after birth are for the mother sacred days of impurity. She has the time and the privacy to experience the sensuous physicality of her relationship with her baby before resuming her share of household responsibilities. This closeness of mother and child is celebrated and reinforced continually in life, and widely expressed in art. No one is more familiar, no one closer, than mother.

Much of the jubilation that accompanies the successful birth arises from relief, just as celebration and thanksgiving follow a successful harvest. The announcement is made to the outside world, the family rejoices, and the whole community welcomes the child.

Overleaf:
p. 108: A mother in the artisan community of Shadipur outside New Delhi comforts her infant as other children look on.

p. 109: Embroidered motifs on a patti-hanging portray a courtyard where children play around the cradle of a newborn child while the mother stands nearby. Such hangings would decorate the door of the house where a child has been born.

Patti-hanging. *Contemporary. Silk embroidery on cloth, 150 x 8" (375 x 19 cm). AIHB Crafts Museum, New Delhi.*

Women friends, kinfolk, and neighbors join to sing of the birth, stitch clothes for the infant, and participate in the cradling ceremony. Gifts are brought—rattles and mobiles to entrance the newborn. The neighborhood children come to peep in on the baby, curious about their new "brother" or "sister." The astrologer may be consulted about the unique configuration of the cosmos which marked this birth. In north India musicians may come to play loudly, to sing and celebrate the arrival. And a group of *hijrā*, or eunuchs come, particularly at the birth of a boy, to claim some payment and bless the child.

Opposite top: Clay figure of a mother massaging her child with oil.

Mother and Child. *Contemporary. Terra cotta, 3¼ x 3¾" (8 x 10 cm). Asutosh Museum of Indian Art, Calcutta.*

Opposite bottom: On the propitious occasion of the birth of a son, the Brāhman priests *(bottom panel)* are called to cast the child's horoscope. Inside the home *(above)* the mother is bathed while the child is suckled, after which the son is presented to his father. *Benares Hindu University, Bharat Kala Bhavan.*

Ritual oil lamps are used in the home for daily worship and special festivals.

Right: Hanging lamp with Gaja-Lakshmī (the goddess Lakshmī being bathed by two elephants).

Hanging Lamp. *Late 18th century. Bronze, 35 x 6" (93 x 16 cm). AIHB Crafts Museum, New Delhi.*

Below left: Yoni-shaped lamp with lingam in the center and Vaishnava symbol on the ornamental handle.
Classical. Hand Lamp. *Mid-19th century. Brass, 3½ x 4¼ x 4¾" (9 x 11 x 12½ cm). Government Museum, Madras.*

Below center: Lamp used in Christian homes with two angels kneeling before a cross.
Classical. Hand Lamp. *Early 19th century. Brass, 7 x 4 x 4¾" (18 x 10½ x 12½ cm). Government Museum, Madras.*

Below right: Lamp with sun and crescent moon symbols.
Hand Lamp. *Late 18th century. Brass, 5¾ x 4¼ x 4¾" (14½ x 11 x 12½ cm). Government Museum, Madras.*

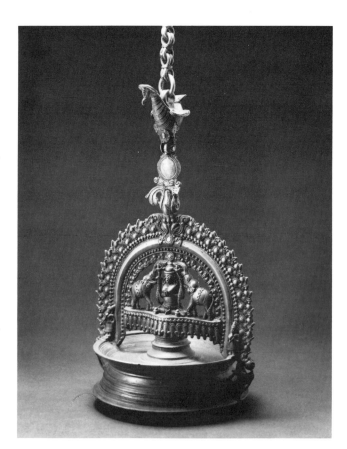

112

Above left: Mango-shaped *pān-dān*, for holding betel (areca) nut, pan leaf, lime, tobacco, cardamon seeds, etc.

Pān-Dān, Betel Leaf and Accessory Container. *Early 20th century. Brass, 3 x 2½ x 2½" (7 x 6 x 6 cm). Rajasthan. Collection of O.P. Jain, New Delhi.*

Above right: A lady's *hukkā* or waterpipe. The mouth piece is inserted in the left-hand socket, the hollow ring is partly filled with water and an earthen pipe bowl is placed on the right-hand socket. Sweetened, aromatic tobaccos are smoked by women as they relax in the privacy of their home.

Hukkā. *Brass. 4 x 3" (10½ x 7 cm). Collection of O.P. Jain, New Delhi.*

Phūlkārī-chādar, bed cover or shawl. Ornamental cloths are woven and embroidered by women of the household to commemorate special occasions such as a child's birth. This contemporary phūlkārī-chādar is from North India.

Right: Festivities in the courtyard of a house can have a boy dressed as a girl to entertain family and friends, since it is not customary for girls to dance for the entertainment of others. Hījrā dancers—eunuchs—also come to the house to bless the newborn boy, to ensure his potency, and to remove the curse which they feel has befallen them.

In Tamil Nadu, for the cradling ceremony, the baby is specially clad and its eyes annointed with *kājal*. The infant's name is traced with a gold coin in a heap of rice onto which the baby is gently lifted, and turned in the direction of the rising sun. He is then girdled protectively with his first sacred thread. Attached to it are five or six gold charms—a mango, a moon, a dog, a champak flower and a fine cylindrical case which holds a prayer for his well-being. The mother whispers the baby's name into his ear for the first time and lifts him into a cradle draped with her wedding sari and hung with garlands.

As the guests admire the child, they leave their gifts in its cradle. The older women begin to sing devotional songs and lullabies that recall the nativity and the cradling of the infant god Krishna.

> *Little body, beautiful as the green hills.*
> *Mouth of coral, lotus eyes.*
> *Oh Krishna undying,*
> *The savour of this blessing!*
> *I want nothing beyond this,*
> *And your blessing!*
> (Traditional Tamil lullaby sung in *Nīlambari-rāga*, the "raga-of-the-blue-sky")[22]

Above: An astrologer contemplates the conjunction of different constellations as he prepares to interpret the infant's horoscope.

The birth of a son is celebrated by drums and loud music.

Left: A woman playing a *dhol*. The skin is painted with the auspicious swastika—the ancient symbol of good luck.

Opposite bottom: An infant in Delhi is carried in a basket lined with soft cloth. Amulets and bracelets serve as adornment and protection.

XI. Safeguarding
the Child

Bathing the baby, massaging it on one's knees, suckling it, dreaming about it in the long still Indian afternoons—this is the stuff of new motherhood. It is a time of sweet lullabies. For every mother, the nativity of her child is *the* nativity. For the Hindu mother, singing to herself as much as to her child, he becomes her Krishna, the playful, curious and amusing child-god.

The child typically grows up surrounded by the affection of two or three generations of the family. The sensuousness and security offered by the mother and the constant presence of other female relatives—grandmother, aunts, sisters and "cousin-sisters"—with their songs, rhythms, and movements, dramatically influence the child during the early years. The father and other male relatives offer assistance and support. It is within a protected world of many people that the child grows. And such protection is needed.

To what kind of world has it come, the
    little one?
For a brief space there is love and light
    and joy.
But the innocent have many enemies,
And near home there can yet be sickness
    and death.
Let the kājal strengthen its eyes against
    them.
Let the name of god be placed next to its
    heart to defend it.
Let this pure iron temper its spirit.
And as we massage it with oils and
    ungruents,
May its limbs grow strong and straight.

Overleaf:
p. 116: Protective Deity on a Horse Preceded by Musicians. *19th century. Brass, 8½ x 6¼" (22½ x 16½ cm). Collection of Pupul Jayakar, New Delhi.*

p. 117: Folk Art, Traditional Style. Shashtī With Babies. *Contemporary. Terra cotta. 6 x 3¾" (15½ x 10 cm). Asutosh Museum of Indian Art, Calcutta.*

The goddess Shashtī, with infants in her arms, is worshipped on the sixth day after the child's birth for protection against infant illnesses.

Opposite: A painted clay image of a deity, surrounded by his warriors and horses, stands along the boundary of a village to protect its inhabitants from evil during the night.

Above:
Painted wooden shutters are commissioned by the householder to show his allegiance to the local chieftain who offers protection to his family.

Window Shutter. *Early 19th century. Rajasthan. Painted wood, 19 x 19⅛" (49 x 50 cm). AIHB Crafts Museum, New Delhi.*

Above: A wandering Sādhu, in the Punjab near Amritsar, dressed as one of the gods, takes a young couple's offering and gives them sacred ashes to heal their infant.

On the festival of Ahoi Ashtamī mothers worship the goddesses Ahoi and Shiau who are protectors of children.

Right: The wall painting depicts the goddess Shiau surrounded by auspicious symbols and her five daughters and sons.

Opposite: A woman massages her infant with oils and herbs to stimulate proper circulation and keep the skin healthy.

Terra cotta figurines of animals are offered to the gods and spirits to protect the child and bring prosperity.

Top left: Camel figure offered to Bhilvat Deo.

Bhil Tribe. Camel. Contemporary. Terra cotta, 14½ x 6½ x 12" (37½ x 18½ x 31 cm). Roopankar, Bharat Bhavan, Bhopal.

Top right: Horse figure offered at the *Nawa* festival to Barā Deo, the great god.

Muria Tribe. Horse. Contemporary. Terra cotta, 14 x 5½ x 15" (36 x 14½ x 39 cm). Roopankar, Bharat Bhavan, Bhopal.

Opposite top: A horse and two buffalo figurines offered to Bhilvat Deo.

Left to right: Horse and Two Buffalos. *Contemporary. Painted terra cotta, 19 × 5½ x 9½" (50 x 14½ x 25 cm), 7 x 3½ x 8" (18 x 9 x 21 cm), 6½ x 3½ x 8" (18 x 9 x 21 cm). Roopankar, Bharat Bhavan, Bhopal.*

Opposite bottom: Bull and Camel. *Contemporary. Terra cotta, Bull: 13 x 5½ x 14" (34 x 14½ x 36 cm); camel: 15 x 6 x 16" (39 x 16 x 39 cm). Roopankar, Bharat Bhavan, Bhopal.*

Elephant—Bastar District. *Contemporary. Terra cotta, 19 x 9½ x 16½ (42 x 21 x 37 cm). Roopankar, Bharat Bhavan, Bhopal.*

During infancy, the child is susceptible to various illnesses and diseases, some thought to be caused by changes of weather, others by the actions of the gods. Medicines—powders, ointments, herbs, and special foods—may be prepared to avert such sickness. Charms and amulets may be needed to ward off the evil eye or the black tongue of a neighbor, jealous of the child and envious of the fortunate mother. Masks may be constructed to dissuade demons from affecting the child. Offerings to guardian dieties such as Aiyanār, the horseman, may be left at shrines to protect the young one against misfortune. Votive offerings may be made to gods and goddesses who control certain types of illness, disease, or misfortune, in order to ward off or avoid such problems. In all, parents, and particularly mothers, attempt to safeguard the child who has been entrusted to them by the gods and who, in its innocence, must be protected and cared for as a god would be.

In the yard there is a pīpal *tree.*
It gives cool shade.
I take this evil on myself, oh mother-goddess
*   Shītalā.*
Beneath its shade my child was playing.
And as he played he took a fever.
I take this evil on myself, oh mother-goddess
*   Shītalā.*
He was crying in distress all night.
All night his mother and his father were afraid.
(Propitiatory song to the smallpox goddess sung at her shrine outside villages in Rajasthan and Gujarat)[23]

Above: A child is made to perform many rituals to appease the gods and keep him healthy. Here a boy stands clothed in protective leaves, his head shaved and anointed with cooling sandalwood paste. In the background are holy Ganges water and offerings to the goddess for protection against illness.

Right: Terra cotta roof tiles decorated with figures of farmer and bull.

Farmer with Plow and Bullock. *Contemporary. Terra cotta; farmer, 8½ x 6 x 12" (22 x 16 x 31 cm); bullock, 7 x 4½ x 14" (18.5 x 12 x 36.1 cm).*

Silver votive plaques of eyes and hands are offered to the deity while praying for a cure as well as after healing has taken place.

Eyes and Hands. *Contemporary. Silver. Eyes, ¾ x 3" (2 x 8 cm); hands, 4¾ x 3" (12 x 8 cm). Government Museum, Madras.*

A mounted warrior, Mokan, is placed at either end of the tiled roof to protect the households of Gond and Oraon tribesmen of Madhya Pradesh from evil.

Roof Tile of "Mokhan" Horse Rider. *Contemporary. Painted terra cotta, 20 x 8½ x 12" (52 x 22 x 31 cm). Roopankar, Bharat Bhawan, Bhopal.*

XII. The Promised World

Conceiving the supporter of the world to be her son,
This ruby among babies,
Smallest of the small,
Unmeasured greatness among the great,
Yashodā rocks the cradle,
And I, Purandaradāsa, look on.
(Cradle song by Purandaradāsa, saint, singer, and originator of the Karnatak musical system, sixteenth century)[24]

Throughout India there is a strong sympathy for the unique inborn temperament and abilities of a child during the early years of infancy. At this time parents are often disposed to follow rather than to lead in dealing with their child's inclinations and tempo of development. The wishes of a young child are often indulged and fulfilled to the extent family resources permit. The unfolding capacities of the child are generally accepted by parents, if not with delight, at least with affectionate tolerance. Cultural traditions and means of play come gradually on their own and are valued for opening up worlds, rather than forcefully molding the growing child.

Overleaf:
p. 126: Singhā, the lion, stands for courage and strength.

Toy from Gujarat. *Contemporary. Wood, painted and lacquered, 8³/₈ x 6¹/₂ x 8″ (22¹/₂ x 16¹/₂ x 20 cm). HHEC, New Delhi.*

p. 127: Horse-drawn cart with movable wheels.

Toy from Gujarat. *Early 20th century. Wood, 17¹/₂ x 8¹/₄ x 6³/₈″ (45¹/₂ x 22 x 17 cm). HHEC, New Delhi.*

In Naga myths, the tiger and man were once equal—until man learned to make fire. A toy tiger is used to reinforce the important role of this animal in traditional culture.

Tiger. *Contemporary. Painted wood, 20½ x 11 x 6" (70 x 29 x 15 cm). AIHB Crafts Museum, New Delhi.*

Kneeling elephant, a symbol of nobility.

Pala School. Kneeling Elephant. *11th century. Bronze, 3½ x 6 x 2¾ (9 x 15½ x 7 cm). Indian Museum, Calcutta.*

Opposite bottom left: Langur monkeys are sacred to the god Hanumān because they helped him rescue Sītā from the demon Rāvana. These toy monkeys are used by children to illustrate this story from the Rāmāyana.

Bandars (Monkeys). *Contemporary.* Iron *(left), 8½ x 4 x 9½ (22 x 10 x 25 cm); (right) 8¼ x 4 x 11" (22 x 10 x 29 cm). Roopankar, Bharat Bhavan, Bhopal.*

Opposite top: Toy seller in Madras with painted wooden animals.

Opposite bottom right: Mother and daughter rag dolls on a swing allow a child to re-create the frivolity of festivals such as Tīj and Baishākī, when young girls swing together and sing songs.

The contemporary artist, Nekchand, famous for his rock garden in Chandigarh, created this image.

130

Opposite left: Marionette puppet show in Delhi with musicians playing the drum and harmonium (hand-pump organ).

Opposite top right: A puppeteer's daughter learns the names and stories of each puppet at an early age and will soon help her parents in the show.

Opposite bottom right: Monkey trainers throughout India provide amusement and education with the help of their costumed monkeys. Here a monkey dressed in women's clothes dances as the trainer relates a story.

Left: A juggler in Shadipur outside Delhi performs for the village children.

Maurya School. Bull. *3rd century* B.C. *Terra cotta, 3½ x 3¾"
(9 x 9½ cm). Benares Hindu
University, Bharat Kala
Bhavan.*

Playthings in India may be exquisitely and intricately wrought of ivory and silver for the sons of kings, or they may be more ephemeral—made of clay and fiber, cane and paper, cotton, feathers, splints of wood, bits of cloth or leftover mirror-work pieces. They may take the form of animals—snakes that suddenly expand, bullocks pulling carts, pecking birds, Bengali shrimp made from pith, horses, elephants, and others. Simple toys which can be bought for small sums in any bazaar or fair and are intended to be enjoyed, wondered at, and thrown away.

Many toys and playthings conjure up the human world. Miniaturized sets of dolls and their accoutrements, and puppets with simple yet elegant movements allow children to recognize, understand, and experiment with human action. Toy-makers, puppeteers, magicians, and others are partners in this, providing the media for the child's discovery and exploration of the world, its constituents and its relationships.

The child's first dolls are traditionally static, easy-to-grasp wood or clay. These figurines may have a startling resemblance to godly icons. This is not surprising, since they are frequently made by the artisans who construct votive figures and craft temple carvings. Playthings thus educate the child, allowing him to recognize the forms and stylized features associated with godly attributes. And the child also learns that a doll is just a doll, and not an icon, unless the image has been made "alive" for worship by the precise ritual act of *prāna-pratishtha* or empowerment.

Ritual objects and children's toys are made by the same artisans and a child soon learns the symbolic importance of certain objects.

Left: Marionette puppet maker carving a female character. Traditional iconographic details identify historical and mythological characters.

Ganesha, the household god and remover of all obstacles, represented above as a child's toy, is an important image that will be repeated throughout a Hindu child's life.

XIII. First Feeding

Widespread throughout India is the notion that a mother's breast milk is a female form of blood. Nurturing an infant is a sacrifice, a transfer of life and vigor, for the child feeds and grows on the blood of its mother. In time, usually relatively late in infancy, the child must be weaned and introduced to solid food. The ability to eat and survive on food produced by adult society signals the end of his nutritional dependence upon his mother.

For the *dvija*, the "twice born" higher castes of India the first feeding is known as *anna-prāshana*, and is celebrated in the sixth month as one of the ancient Hindu samskāras. The first mouthful of food is the traditional and auspicious mixture of sweet rice, clarified butter, and milk. Offerings are made to the sacred fire and the goddess of speech. Accompanying prayers invoke life, vitality, and the purification of all senses through which nourishment is received.

Anna-prāshana, like other samskāras, is a religious rite which seeks to cleanse, sanctify, and refine the nature of the person. The food ingested by the child is thought to affect not only his physical nature, but also his psychological and moral character. The proper consumption of more sublime and subtle foods, including *prasād*—foods infused with divine essences—is said to make one a better, more refined human being.

As the child begins to eat, he learns the dietary rules and norms of his caste. He experiences the humoral qualities of food. And he learns of those who may and may not feed him—something which will be continually elaborated throughout his life.

Overleaf: Copper imitation of a conch shell baby feeder or ritual libation vessel. An infant is fed with milk and rice water by gently inserting the spout to the side of the mouth. The ritual purity of the conch shell insures good health and prosperity for the child.

Baby Feeder. *19th century. Copper, cast and chased, 1¹⁄₂ x 2³⁄₄ x 5″ (6¹⁄₂ x 7 x 13 cm). Indian Museum, Calcutta.*

Above: Traditional measures for grain. A child's first solid food is usually rice or wheat.

Grain Measures. *19th century. Brass, left: 9 x 5″ (25 x 13 cm); right: 16 x 3¹⁄₂″ (42 x 8¹⁄₂ cm). Collection of O.P. Jain, New Delhi.*

Opposite top: Ritual first feeding is often done at the temple. A Brāhman priest of the Guruvayur Temple, Trichur, ladles out sweet rice, bread, fruit, and sweets that were first offered to the god Krishna. Among the Nairs of Kerala, the boy's maternal uncle feeds him first, then the rest of the family takes turns.

Left: Traditional food categories and their appropriate use are explained through the age-old principles of *Ayurvedic* medicine or *Yunani tib*. This Ayurvedic booklet outlines the types of food that should be eaten at different seasons by different individuals; men or women, young or old.

Above: Food containers from the Nicobar Islands. *Left: Contemporary.* Palm spathe and bamboo, 5¾ x 7½ x 7¼" (15 x 19½ x 19 cm). *Right:* Serving dish from Nagaland. *Contemporary. Bamboo, 3¼ x 6½ x 10½" (8 x 17 x 27 cm).*

Large clay water pot, decorated with auspicious floral motifs.

Decorated Earthen Pitcher. *Late 19th century. Clay terra cotta, 12½ x 13" (33 x 34 cm). Indian Museum, Calcutta.*

Despite the seriousness with which Indian parents attempt to feed their young and the efforts of Indian craftsmen to design appropriate eating utensils for infants, children, as the paradigmatic godchild Krishna, approach the activity with a mischievous and playful abandon that sometimes captures the essence of being alive and experiencing a new world.

Yashodā sees the stolen butter smeared on the face of child Krishna:
Oh Krishna child
Come quickly,
Show me your face . . .

Yashodā hears that Krishna has eaten dirt:
Oh Krishna child
Come quickly,
Open your mouth . . .

Then he showed his mother
The whole world in his mouth . . .
Oh Krishna child
Come quickly,
Show me your face . . .
(Devotional song by Purandaradāsa, frequently enacted in the classical dance *bhārata nātyam*)[25]

Two examples of a lotā, or water pot, one brass, one bell metal, used for dipping water or bathing.

Above: Lotā. *Contemporary. Brass, 3 x 4" (8 x 10½ cm). Collection of Francis Wacziarg, New Delhi.*

Left: Lotā. *19th century. Bell metal, 4¼ x 3¼" (9 x 8½ cm). Benares Hindu University, Bharat Kala Bhavan.*

XIV. The First Step

"*Thumaka-thumaka*" is the sound of the faintly jingling bells of the anklets traditionally placed on the child in order to delight him as he attempts his first steps. It is the sound of the footsteps of the child Rāma, celebrated in devotional song throughout India. As the child struggles to walk and explore the world he is aided by people and objects around him. Parents, relatives, and especially older siblings provide guidance and encouragement. Crafted aids, including walking and push carts, provide firm support. Some of these, exquisitely carved and designed, suggest Krishna's chariot, reinforcing the identification between child and god.

Sweet the speaking,
Sweet the doing,
Sweet the wearing,
Sweet the stance,
Sweet in going,
Sweet in roaming,
Honey sweet,
The honeyed Lord.
("The Eight Honeyed Lines on Lord Krishna," by Vallabhāchārya, scholar and teacher of the "Way of Grace," Gokul, fifteenth century)[26]

Overleaf: Terra cotta figure of baby Krishna crawling.

Child Krishna. *19th century. Terra cotta, 15½ x 5" (40 x 13 cm). Collection of Francis Wacziarg, New Delhi.*

Opposite: A child's first steps are supported by a wheeled walker and guided by his mother's protective foot.

XV. Initiation Into Learning

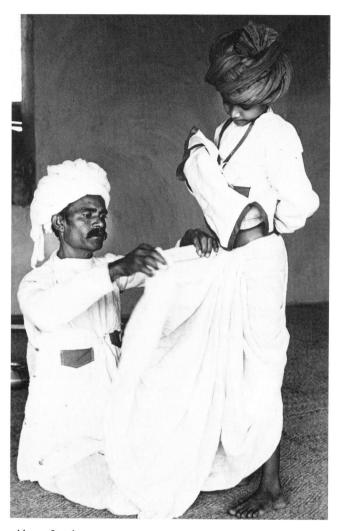

Above: It takes many years of patient instruction before a boy masters the etiquette of dress and behavior. Rajasthani father and son.

Opposite: Walking along the beach near Puri, on the Bay of Bengal, a woman and her daughter are going to collect the fish for market.

Overleaf: In the guiding hands of the mother, a young girl offers sacred Ganges water at Varanasi to the god Sūrya the sun.

Even
A waterjar
Is filled
Drop
By falling drop.
(Dhammapada 9:7, Buddhist text, c. 400-200 B.C.)[27]

Indian children are not separated from adult society—rather, they are encouraged to participate in it as curious yet respectful apprentices. The child is not considered a hindrance by his parents and kinspeople, who are his first teachers. Girls may play in the courtyard and also attempt to help their mothers in processing and preparing foods under the watchful eyes of older female relatives. A boy, once old enough and out of the care of his mother, may follow his father to the fields, a workshop, or a village temple.

The Hindu child begins to learn the *dharma*, or code of conduct, for his caste. If the child of a Brāhman, the priestly caste, he learns of the holy and scholarly treatises kept by his family, hears the ancient Sanskrit chants of his elders, and becomes aware of the ritually purifying services provided by his family to other villagers. If born to a warrior caste, the ancient Kshatriyas, or contemporary Rajputs, he learns of the martial traditions embodied in family weaponry and of the honor and responsibility of governance observed as villagers march into his father's sitting room. If born to a merchant or artisan caste, included in the ancient Vaishya category, the child may be exposed to account books, storerooms of provisions, workplaces, and specialized technical knowledge. And if born into one of the Shūdra castes, he learns of its particular pattern of action and begins to form a notion of how he is to behave in his dealings with others.

A Muslim, Christian, Sikh, Buddhist, Jain, Parsi or Jewish child also learns, first from his or her family and later through visits to places of worship and through teachers, the expected way.

From early childhood a
potter's daughter becomes
familiar with the clay that
will be her livelihood.

In addition to parents, kinfolk, and formal
instructors, the child is served by other teachers—
artisans, musicians, and itinerant performers who
convey and make real through their art knowledge
of nature, history, language, and the gods. The
street magician, the monkey trainer, and the snake
charmer pass through the town or village, attract-
ing the child alive in everyone. Such events are
educational as well as entertaining. The juggler
from Andhra Pradesh not only enthralls his audience with feats of the balancing top and sword-
swallowing, but also conveys the movements and
the spirit of the monkey god Hanumān, whom he
explicitly is said to imitate. The mendicant singer
with his single-stringed instrument tells of ancient
heroes and extolls devotion to the gods.

In Orissa, Bengal, Gujarat, and Rajasthan, pic-
ture-showing bards unwind their scrolls of paintings like a scroll of time or hold up their painted
cards. The balladeers from Rajasthan, a male *bhopā*
and female *bhopī*, display their hand-painted story
scroll, and while illuminating the panels retell the
well-aged tales of warrior heroes and heroines. The
night is rich for the child hearing the alluring song
of the *bhopī*, the rhythmic stamping of the *bhopā's*
ankle bells, and the plaintive call of the stringed
rāvanahatta punctuated by their long desert cries.

I greet
With honor
Those
Who know.
(Phrase to be written and read by the child when
initiated into learning)[29]

Left: Rajasthani balladeer
Ram Karan Bhopā teaches
his son Shish Ram to play
the many-stringed
rāvanahatta.

Below: A young boy learns
to color the story scroll that
is used by balladeers in
Rajasthan.

Above left: A Mughal miniature of the 18th century shows a group of acrobats performing dangerous feats with swords and daggers.

Acrobatic Performance. *1700-1725, provincial Mughal. Painting on paper, 11 x 7½" (29 x 19½ cm) without tapestry border, 14¾ x 11" (38 x 29 cm). National Museum, New Delhi.*

Above right: Modern tightrope walker attracts evening strollers on Chowpathy Beach, Bombay.

Opposite top: A ferocious Himalayan black bear grapples with its trainer while villagers look on in wonder and amusement.

Opposite bottom: Even before she learns to walk, a snake charmer's daughter learns not to fear the poisonous cobra.

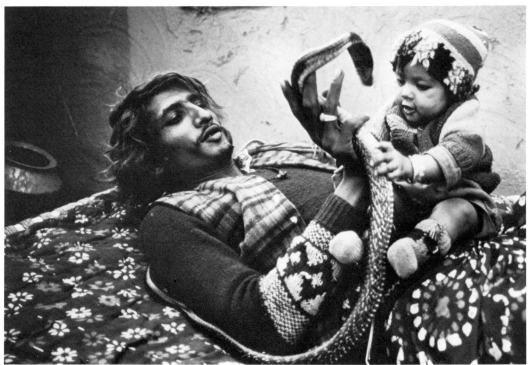

In wealthy families, the six-year-old child's hand is ceremonially guided through saffron scattered on silver. For most Hindus, it is traced in an auspicious heap of rice. The resulting letters are inevitably large and lacking in grace, but this first writing and reading marks the child's initiation into the literate world of his culture's great traditions.

This ceremony entails the presence of gods, parents, and one's *guru*, or teacher, who embodies the characteristics of both god and parent. The child is bathed and, after propitiating the household deities, honors the various godly patrons of learning—Ganesha, the elephant-headed god and remover of obstacles; Sāvitrī, the sun and enlightener; Brihaspatī, the teacher of the gods; and Sarasvatī, the goddess of speech, poetry, and music. In the presence of honored relatives and guests, the child writes "aum," the sound of the universe, and a salutation to the gods and those who have already walked the path of knowledge. The child reads what he has written three times to his guru. The guru is circumambulated three times and given appropriate gifts.

Above: At the Jami Masjid of Fatehpur Sikri a small girl joins the congregation in the observance of Id prayers. Traditionally, Muslim women pray separately from the men.

Right: The sons and daughters of Gujār nomads learn to read and write in an outdoor government school. They write on slate boards with a wooden pen dipped in white clay. Once they learn the script, they can use pen and paper.

Above: Elaborate brass pen cases and inkwells were often presented to a nobleman's son when he began his first writing lesson.

Brass Pen Cases and Inkwells. *Contemporary. From left to right: 12 x 5 x 2" (32 x 13½ x 5 cm); 14 x 3" (36 x 8 cm); 5 x 3" (13½ x 8 cm); 12 x 5½" (32 x 14 cm); 4 x 3½" (10½ x 9 cm); foreground: 2 x 1¾ x 1½" (5 x 5 x 4 cm). Collection of Francis Wacziarg, New Delhi.*

Top: This permanently painted learning board or *takhtī* from Gujarat provides a lesson that the student must copy. At the top is the image of Ganesha, who is propitious for all beginnings, being fanned by a worshipper. *Collection of Pupul Jayakar, New Delhi.*

Above: In the shaded portico of the Ramnagar Palace, A Brāhman priest instructs these boys in religion, philosophy, and politics, based on ancient Sanskrit texts.

Right: Portable shrine of the Mother Goddess and a mask worn by the story-teller-priest who serves her. Not all people can afford to travel to the holy Ganges, but for a few grains of rice and some money, they can view the Goddess and be purified all the same.

Mother Goddess Shrine from Andhra Pradesh. Early 20th century. *Painted wood, 20½ x 16¼ (64 x 42 cm). AIHB Crafts Museum, New Delhi.*

Below: Throughout north India, during the Rām-Līlā or Dassehrā festival, giant images of the demon King Rāvana (center) and his brother demons are erected with bamboo cane and paper. They are finally burned to celebrate Rāma's victory and his freeing of Sītā.

Opposite top left: A traveling storyteller helps his wife to set down his picture box. Inside are painted panels that can be opened and unfolded as he relates the various legends and myths. Two images of the goddess Lakshmī sitting on a lotus appear on the top panels.

Opposite bottom left: A bahrūpiyā, man "with many forms," is seen dressed as a Langur monkey, mischievously eating some stolen watermelon.

Opposite bottom right: Bahrūpiyā. *Early 18th century. Gouache on paper. Miniature. Benares Hindu University, Bharat Kala Bhavan.*

The teachers of traditional India are highly regarded for their knowledge and personal commitment to their disciples. The relationship approximates that of master and apprentice in that it extends beyond any classroom or particular context. Students typically live in the households of their teachers, perform diverse tasks for them, and solicit and receive various forms of aid. Beyond this, the relationship takes on a religious or godly character, for teachers bestow blessings, knowledge, wisdom, and livelihood. The gurus of Hindus and Sikhs and the ustāds of Muslims are all those who teach, whether their subject is yoga, mathematics, literature, juggling, magic, or automotive repair. The common thread is a respect for knowledge, a reverent honoring of the knower, and a parent-child relationship—replete with love, nurturance, and personal concern—between teacher and student.

XVI. Learning To Be
and To Do

*No, it is not easy in all three worlds
To find a teacher like the alchemist's stone
To turn a student's raw ore into gold.
How much more precious then,
Is one who turns the other not just to gold
But to his very likeness—
That which transmutes others still, and others into
   gold.*
(Attributed to Sankarāchārya, theologican-
philosopher and founder of a Hindu monastic
order, Kerala, 700-800 A.D.)[30]

The transmission of knowledge in traditional
India is from one to one to another through time.
It is a matter of child learning from parent, student
from teacher, apprentice from master—and then in
turn, children becoming parents, students becoming teachers, and apprentices becoming masters.

The traditional relationship between teacher and
learner or *guru* and *shishya* is marked by an initiation ceremony—the *upanayana*—which establishes
the bond between the two as that of a second
birth—the gateway to a new life, that of the knowledgeable adult. Done as a samskāra by those of the
twice-born castes—Brāhmans, Kshatriyas, and
Vaishyas—the ceremony is marked by the investiture of the sacred thread to be worn across the
upper body and instruction in the ritual privileges
of ancient Hinduism. This period of instruction is
followed by the entrance of the male student into
the community of householders as a responsible
and capable member of society.

Overleaf p. 156: A family
troupe of acrobats heads
for Chowpathy beach in
Bombay where they will
perform until dusk.

p. 157: Two Brāhman boys
learn the scriptures and
sacred rituals by helping
their father who performs
ceremonies for pilgrims at
Varanasi.

158

Opposite top: An intricate plaque used for worship in the home or worn to prevent illness. The main subject is Hanumān carrying herbs to heal the wounded Lakshmana. At the top is Balarāma, Krishna's brother, and at bottom the baby Krishna is shown with a ball of ghee or clarified butter in his hand.

19th century. Brass, 8½ x 7" (22 x 18 cm). AIHB Crafts Museum, New Delhi.

Opposite bottom: A Parsi school in Bombay where boys are taught the sacred teachings of Zarathustra (Zoroaster).

Left: After receiving the sacred thread, a Brāhman youth is expected to observe many social and religious rules.

A boy in Varanasi
stops at a roadside shrine
to the god Hanumān, mak-
ing an offering for courage
and strength.

Above left: Gaja-Lakshmī, the goddess of wealth and prosperity.

Gaja-Lakshmi, C. *17th century. Bell metal. Collection of Pupul Jayakar, New Delhi.*

Above: The goddess Kālī dancing on the body of Shiva is a reminder of the power of tantric energy.

Kālī Dancing on Shiva. *3½ x 3½ x 2″ (9 x 9 x 5 cm). Lance Dane Collection at Sanskriti Museum.*

Left: Ritual scenario made on an engine fan blade depicts Shiva in the form of a linga, Ganesha, his son, Nandī the bull, and two humans, one of whom is a snake charmer.

Shiva Linga, Nandī, Ganesha and Two Worshippers. *Contemporary. Steel, 5¼ x 4¼ x 2″ (14 x 11 x 5 cm). Collection of Lance Dane, Bombay.*

161

Such relationships survive even beyond the purview of the twice-born Hindus. To become a *chitrakār* in Bengal, a Muslim boy learns to paint *patuā* story scrolls and sing mythological tales and tribal histories under the tutelage of his ustād, usually an elder male relative. The boy learns to make his own paints from natural materials—yellow from turmeric, blue from indigo, orange from vermillion, purple from spinach leaves, and black from burnt rice—and to make his own brushes from goat hair. With his guru he travels from village to village, learning to narrate and sing his stories, to capture the heart and imagination of his audience. In early adulthood he supports his family and assumes the responsibility for their care, secure in his knowledge that the path he travels is honorable and worthwhile.

Girls, too, learn from their teachers, often elder kinswomen who educate them in home crafts. Developing skill in embroidery and weaving may be oriented to the accumulation of dowry, but it also serves the needs of the household economy and cottage industry.

Above: While a mother babysits one child, her other daughter learns to weave intricate mats used for prayer and sitting.

Opposite: A young image maker in Bengal prepares an image of the goddess Durgā for the annual festival of Durgāpūjā.

Above: School girls visiting the Belur temple, Karnataka, receive a lesson in ancient mythology.

Opposite: A storekeeper in Aurangabad, Maharashtra, teaches his grandson reading and mathematics.

The coming of age for a girl has no corresponding samskāra to that of upanayana for a boy. Referred to as *kumārī phūl*, the flowering of maidenhood, it is marked by menarche, the natural signal of womanhood. In south India, it is celebrated with feasting and gladness, but most communities observe it quietly. Afterward, the girl will be expected to bear greater responsibility for her actions and her parents will be more vigilant. Marriage offers will be made. In the villages of western Rajasthan she wears a rose-colored, tie-dyed veil on the way to the village well. Already a new life cycle is being prepared for and anticipated.

Above: A young potter sells pots at the Baneshwar melā in Rajasthan.

Opposite: Young acrobats in Shadipur, outside of New Delhi.

167

XVII. Fairs and Festivals

Maharaja Ram Singh playfully squirts the ladies with colored water during the festival of Holi.

Maharaja Ram Singh Celebrating Holi. *Late 18th century. Paint on paper, 21½ x 29" (56 x 74½ cm). Benares Hindu University, Bharat Kala Bhavan.*

The snake boat race is a traditional event of the Onam Festival and all are invited to participate.

Overleaf p. 168: Rajasthani girl at a country fair.

p. 169: Gujarati women pilgrims at Dwarka dance and sing praises to Krishna.

Each of India's many religious groups, sects, and communities—Hindus, Muslims, Christians, Sikhs, Buddhists, Jains, Parsis, and Jews—and others all have their holy days, days of celebration and remembrance. Many of these festivals link the home with the outside world. They may be tied to the agricultural cycle and the household work cycle, and hence be celebrated after harvesting has been completed, or before sowing is necessary. The foods prepared and served at such festivals also follow the seasons and the crops grown.

Festivals in India are frequently celebrations of exemplary cosmological, social, or personal victories. Typically, the core of a festival involves ritual activities through which the exploits of gods, goddesses, heroes, heroines, gurus, prophets, saints, and leaders are brought to life.

In a rural setting in Rajasthan a young man squirts colored water on his cousin's wife.

For the ten days of the Onam Festival in Kerala, the *athapu* flower arrangement is built a layer a day. Children receive new clothes and go to worship in the temple.

Powdered color merchant in Mysore sets out his stock for Holi. On the first day of Holi only dry colors are used, but on the second day wet colors and other substances are all fair game.

171

Right: Giant images of bamboo and paper are constructed for the Rām-līlā in Ramnagar.

Below: Ten-headed Rāvana mask used in the Rām-līlā, when the major events of the Rāmāyana epic are enacted. *AIHB Crafts Museum, New Delhi.*

Opposite top left: At the sacred shrine of Shravana Belgola in Mysore, the Jain saint Gomatesvāra receives a special anointing of precious substances including gems, gold, and silver. Every 12 or 15 years Jain priests anoint the 17-meter (57-foot tall) image.

Opposite top right: Once a year at the Ratha Yātra, the chariot festival, the image of Lord Jagannātha is carried at Puri in a massive chariot pulled by thousands of devotees.

For Hindus, the activation of icons makes present the power of the various deities represented. This presence is transmitted to festival sponsors and audience by *darshan*, or viewing the icons, by *pūjā*, or worshipping the deity, by eating *prasād*, food permeated with the god's power, or by love or service to the god as indicated by singing his praises, dancing, engaging in a drama, and other means. By participating in this way, festival-makers and -goers are marked by the presence of exemplary figures, becoming more like gods and goddesses and hence better people.

Among Muslims in India, a similar type of marking occurs by partaking of the *barkat* or blessedness of an exemplary *pīr* or saint, invoking the exploits of the prophet, or chanting the verses of the holy Quran. Among Sikhs, this occurs through imbibing specially blessed food and divine nectar (amrit), and the donning of certain clothing to emulate one's gurus.

A trinket stall at the Baneshwar Melā attracts customers with an array of colorful ornaments, jewelry, and cosmetics.

This marking process allows for further growth. It links the human being to a higher and exemplary moral authority and also allows for the further elaboration and unity of human communities through that authority. Festivals reinforce the pattern of childhood in that they bring the gods close and bind the individual to the community. Both functions are fulfilled by the artisans, craftspeople, and performers who, in their display of creativity and their transmission of the traditional, enable what is for Indians the process of life.

In India, the *melā* or fair is often a religious festival. Melās bring together ritual functionaries, artisans, craftspeople, dancers, musicians, speech-makers, dramatists, itinerant performers, sideshow operators, food vendors, merchandise hawkers, and throngs of parents and children. A fair provides the opportunity for people from different villages, towns, and regions to meet and mix with others. It brings into contact people of various castes, classes, backgrounds, and interests. Such people mix in a way not usually possible in the isolation and relative homogeneity of their own home, neighborhood, or social group. The word *melā* is itself derived from the Sanskrit root "mil," denoting a meeting and mixing. At a fair, this mixing occurs by seeing each other, joining in processions, worshipping together, forming an audience for performances, eating food from a common kitchen, breathing common air, hearing the same sounds.

Above left: Walking together, a group of women from one village head for the Baneshwar Melā. They will make their purchases as a group, as well as eat, sing, and dance together.

Left: Camping in the open at the Pushkar Melā, nomad women prepare food, surrounded by their cattle, sheep, buffalos, and camels. Pushkar is one of the few places in India where the god Brahmā is worshipped at a shrine, but of equal attraction are the livestock shows and trading.

A melā brings together society and articulates it in geographical, cosmological, and historical settings. The time of a melā is set by the motions and positions of the stars, moon, and planets. The location is set by the concurrence of rivers, streams, and the trade routes of caravans. The particular site is determined by the activities of the gods, heroes, and saints. And like other events throughout the life cycle in India, the melā provides an experience that highlights the richness and interconnectedness of life itself.

Opposite top: Once every twelve years the Kumbha Melā is held at Hardwar to commemorate the triumph of the gods over the demons when they captured the *kumbha*, the pot filled with immortal nectar. This melā is held on alternate years at Hardwar, Ujjain, Nasik, and Prayag (Allahabad). At Prayag, where the sacred Ganga, Jamuna, and heavenly Saraswati rivers meet, the Kumbha Melā is attended by as many as 11 million people, making it the largest fair in India.

Opposite bottom: Dīwālī, the Festival of Lights, centers on the worship of Lakshmī—the goddess of wealth, and prosperity. These housewives from an upperclass Delhi household quietly prepare the altar to the goddess in the home, while outside the skies are filled with rockets and firecrackers.

Left: On Ganesha Chaturthī, the birthday of the god Ganesha, thousands of clay images are adorned with flowers and offerings of fruits and sweets. This image in Bombay will soon be taken to the beach to be immersed.

Moving Out

The villager looks ahead and the city dweller remembers:

> *That red earth path*
> *Leading out of the village,*
> *Leaving it behind;*
> *Oh just to think of it, brother,*
> *And I'm lost to myself.*
> ("Song of the Way," Rabindranath Tagore, poet, painter, musician, educator, and Nobel Prize laureate from Bengal, twentieth century)[31]

Beyond the somewhat protected environment of the home lies the vastness of India—the richness of its temples and pilgrimage sites, the colorfulness of its bazaars, the congestion of its cities, the fragrances of its high valleys, and the liveliness of its roads and byways.

From worshipping at sacred shrines to trading goods in far-off markets, the child becoming an adult makes his or her way away from the home to discover how similar and how different others are. One learns of new gods and goddesses, eats their holy food, and comes to know them. New cloth is worn, new foods tasted, new arts experienced. And through discovery of the new, the old—even the ancient—is learned. An Indian watching acrobats perform in the street, replete with what seem like modern devices, can observe in the twisting and handstands of small girls the retention and preservation of the ancient yogic *āsana* or poses.

Boys growing into men discover new worlds in councils, courts, banks, and congeries of modern institutions. Women, too, through schools, jobs, community associations, and visits to relatives, move beyond the village or town neighborhood, and add more to the life experiences they have been taught.

And even with a shift to the city, there is the continual rediscovery of the village. Even the most urbane Indian refers to "my village." These links

Above: Afternoon sun filters through the coconut palms as an oxcart driver in Tamil Nadu urges his bullocks on.

Opposite: Mother and child on the beach at Mahabalipuram in Tamil Nadu.

to the past, to the village, and to rich folk traditions provide a certain centeredness which not only balances, but incorporates disruption and dissonance. The Indian child has learned that the divine is always near, evidenced in food to eat, crafts, paintings, and nature itself. The child also learns that he is a part of a specific community, inextricably tied to others from a time even before his own conception. This centeredness, like the object of the craftsmen's labor, is created carefully with a sense of respect for the divinity it invokes, and the strength it provides for the future.

If your soul is no stranger to you,
The whole world is your home.
(Kabir, weaver, mystic, and integrator of Hinduism and Islam, and esteemed in Sikhism, Benares, fifteenth century)[32]

Contemporary India stretches from the glaciers of the high Himalayas, through deserts, to palmlined tropical coasts. It hosts the past wealth of maharajas, the poverty of urban beggars, and the resources of a cosmopolitan elite. India is home to more than 750 million people speaking at least twenty-six different languages and worshipping the gods of all major religions. It spans the ancient world of an early civilization, a period of colonial conquest and rule, and the current context of Third World politics. It combines the tight-knit agricultural world of the village with the highly technical one of the growing megalopolis. And India incorporates the traditions which have come alive in the last five thousand years with those in the making. In this, India is tremendously diverse. And yet, in the exploration occasioned by fairs, pilgrimages, and travels, as in the wonder of the child excited by the skill of the craftsman, there is the opportunity to share with others, to appreciate, and to come together in the celebration of life: *Aditi.*

Overleaf:
Durgāpūjā is celebrated with great passion all over India. Neighborhoods vie with each other to create original and spectacular pūjā pandāls (enclosures) and images, ranging in style from traditional to calendar art imitations complete with electronic "disco" lights.

p.180: As it has been practiced for generations, Durgāpūjā is celebrated in this large courtyard of a private home.

p.181: In a public ceremony a Brāhman priest officiates before the image of Durgā slaying the buffalo demon.

p.182-183:
At the Puram (festival) of Trichur, Kerala in May, processions from nearby temples pay homage at the Vadakanātha (Shiva) temple. In friendly rivalry, two major temples each parade fifteen richly caparisoned elephants. To the sound of drums and loud music, priests seated on the elephants display silk and brocade parasols, yak tail whisks, and peacock feather fans to honor the deity who is enshrined in a golden arch on the center elephant. Nightlong processions and a fireworks display at dawn conclude the festivities.

The Role of Myth
in the Indian Life Cycle
Wendy Doniger O'Flaherty

Introduction: Life and Myths

We in the West generally assume a sharp dualistic division between myth and reality, and a corresponding dichotomy between God and man. We define "myth" as Plato taught us to define it, as a story that is not true, in contrast with, for instance, history or science, which are true. But in India, these categories tend to dissolve into one another; "the myth of marriage," does not mean "a false image of marriage," let alone "a lie about marriage," but rather "a story about the marriage of the gods that reveals to us what human marriage is *really* about, even when it appears to be about something else." The Indian vocabulary has no word for myth. Instead, scholars use the words *dīvya-kathā* or divine story, and *purā-kathā* or ancient tale interchangeably. For myth and reality in Hindu India are such identical twins that it is often impossible to tell them apart. So, too, our Western assumption that gods are quintessentially different from humans is quickly challenged by Indian mythology, in which gods generally succumb to the weaknesses that plague us; the primary difference between gods and humans is that the gods live in heaven, and that they live much longer than we do (though not, in fact, forever; they are "immortal" only in a very vague sort of a way, since *no one*, not even the gods, survives the fires and floods of the recurrent doomsdays that punctuate infinity).

And not only are the gods close to us in their nature; they are physically close to us in India, present on earth in incarnations or in disguised forms. Hindus feel intimate with their gods, able to address them and to offer them not only awestruck worship but small creature comforts: they feed their gods (as these appear in the form of metal or stone images in houses and temples), and then distribute the leftovers to the devotees (as *prasāda* or blessed food). They change their clothes, and fan them in the hot weather, and swing them on swings, and scratch their backs with specially sanctified back-scratchers. As evidence of the fact that the gods are so like us and come so much among us that it is hard to tell whether one is in the presence of a human or a god, certain texts offer five ways in which one may tell by looking at someone whether he or she is mortal or immortal: the gods never blink or sweat; their garlands never wither nor do their clothes become dusty; and their feet never quite touch the ground, but hover slightly about it.

The myths, therefore, constantly remind Hindus how close they are to all the gods of the pantheon; but some are closer than others, or, rather, are close in different ways. Many Hindu divinities appear on earth as people (or, sometimes, as animals) in particular villages; but the great gods are always present everywhere. In the ancient, Vedic period, it was the Creator who was omnipresent in this way; sometimes he was given no name; sometimes he was called Prajāpati, "Lord of Creatures," or Brahmā, "religious power incarnate." Later, "he" became "it," as Brahmā became the neuter name *brahman*, the godhead, the world-soul that is identical with the individual soul or *ātman*.

To this day, Hindus believe that their souls are a part of the soul of the godhead, and this makes them "close" to god in a very particular and intense way: they *are* god. The "infinity" of this sort of god may lie behind the name of the goddess Aditi; and it is possible that she was once worshipped as the living, anthropomorphic form of the impersonal godhead. But Aditi is no longer worshipped as an image in India. Instead, Hindus worship a number of other gods who tend to be identified with one of the two principal male gods—Vishnu and Shiva. There are, in addition, a number of female divinities who are often identified with Devī (the Goddess), but these, too, tend to be associated with one or the other of the two main streams defined by the male gods, as the goddesses are usually said to be related in some way (often, though not always, through marriage) to either Vishnu or Shiva.

The relationship between life and myth is a chicken-and-egg relationship, or, as the Indians put it, a seed-and-tree relationship: each gives rise to the other. Myths told to children influence how they grow up; children grow up with certain cultural preoccupations that lead them to tell certain myths. G. Morris Carstairs, a psychiatrist who worked in India, spoke of shared "nuclear phantasies" that were transmitted in India from mother to child and later modified by individual experience; he went on to suggest that these infantile fantasies are often expressed in myths. But he also argued that certain myths about the goddess that were expressed in rituals that children witnessed may have been the source of the feelings that these children later experienced toward human women. Thus the myth may be both a cause and a result of an actual life situation.[1]

Nor are encounters with human beings the only source of experiential counterparts to myths; animals often reveal the gods, as their vehicles and as manifestations of their power. For instance, the elephant of Indra symbolizes his sovereign position among the gods and his control over rain, for the elephant is a symbol of royalty and fertility. Animals and gods are the two communities poised on the frontiers of the human community, the two others by which we define our-

Modern chalk art of Shiva on the wall of an ornate alcove depicts the more popular symbols of the god; lingam, trident, damaru drum, serpent, etc.

selves; and whether or not people get the gods they deserve, they tend to get the gods their animals deserve. The natural flora and fauna of any country have a lot to do with the ways in which the people of that country perceive their gods. Thus, the ingenious mischievousness of the monkey and the uncanny cruelty and beauty of the tiger, two of the outstanding inhabitants of the Indian jungle, have found their way into the images of many Hindu gods and goddesses.

The Myth of Coming of Age

In classical Hindu social theory—which is still alive and well and living in India—the members of the adult community are called "twice-born" (*dvija*, a term that also designates a bird or a tooth, both of which are, in different senses, born again). The first birth is the birth from the mother, but the second, more important birth takes place through the formal initiation in which the young man receives the sacred thread that ties him to all other Hindus who have ever been or ever will be. The myths about this experience express many of the powerful emotions that the ritual itself does not spell out. Paul Courtright has argued that the myth of the god Ganesha is, among other things, a myth of initiation.[2] Ganesha is born from the dirt that Pārvatī washes off her body; she places him at the door of her bathroom to keep her husband out; the husband, who is the god Shiva, beheads Ganesha and eventually replaces his head with that of an elephant.[3] Courtright points out the striking resemblances between elements of this myth and the ceremony of the boy's initiation (*upanayana*): when Ganesha's mother makes him out of the dirt of her body, her role is similar to that of the boy's mother who smears him with turmeric; when Ganesha's mother places him on guard in the doorway she separates him from herself; Ganesha's beheading and resuscitation by his father are parallel to the cutting of the young man's hair in the ceremony and his re-birth into the new life. Thus the myth of Ganesha expresses the boy's separation from his mother, his initiation through symbolic mutilation by a new "father" (the preceptor or *āchārya* who performs the ceremony of initiation), and the arduous acculturation necessary to make the young man truly a person in the adult world. The myth of Ganesha can be fully understood only in the context of the general process and the specific ritual of male initiation in India, but the participants in that process and in that ritual come to understand the meaning of initiation in part through their thorough familiarity with the myth of Ganesha.

Many other well-known Indian myths have served for centuries as paradigms through which young men have understood their own initi-

Shiva and Pārvatī with Nandī.

Shiva and Pārvatī with Nandī. *Contemporary. Painted papier mâché, 7 x 5 x 3" (18¼ x 13 x 8 cm). HHEC Collection, New Delhi.*

ation. When the god Vishnu becomes incarnate as the cowherd Krishna, he kills his wicked uncle, Kamsa, as soon as he reaches manhood; in doing this, Krishna re-enacts a primeval Oedipal confrontation that is the counterpart of Ganesha's encounter with his father; but this time, the young man strikes the final blow. The trials of exile and the triumphant return to the throne of Rāma, the hero of the epic Rāmāyana, function both as a personal initiation (for Rāma, too, is injured by his father, who allows him to be unjustly exiled) and as a political ceremony of royal consecration. Thus, in very different ways, and with many different meanings—religious meanings, psycho-sexual meanings, philosophical meanings—these stories express the pain and the ultimate victory that the male child experiences in fighting his way out of childhood into manhood. Indian boys know these stories well, and use them in constructing their own self-images and expectations.

Papier-mâché sculpture of the wedding of Rāma and Sītā.

The Myth of Marriage

But what of the young girl? What of her transition into womanhood? Although there is no formal ceremony of initiation for a woman at the time of puberty, according to the classical system this period generally coincides with the moment of her marriage; and marriage certainly does serve as the initiation of the girl into womanhood. Myths, through the millennia, connect human brides to an ancient heritage, which is reaffirmed in every marriage ceremony, as verses from ancient hymns are chanted by the officiating priest. There is one particular myth and ritual of marriage that spans the entire spectrum from the earliest records of Indo-Aryan civilization in India, for it is preserved in a hymn from the Rig Veda, composed around 1200 B.C., and is still used in marriage ceremonies in India today. Moreover, this text provides a striking example of the complex manner in which myth and life interact in rites of passage. It is worth looking at in detail and at length.

The forty-seven verses of the hymn (Rig Veda 10.85) function on at least three distinct levels, which are not segregated into different sections of the hymn but are constantly interleaved. The first level describes the marriage of Sūryā, the daughter of the sun, to Soma, the moon. In this paradigmatic sacred wedding, the wedding chariot was the chariot of the sun, with the sky for its canopy and songs of praise for its shafts (vv. 8-10). But halfway through the telling of this story, the hymn moves to a second level of diction and begins to exhort the human bride, who is addressed as Sūryā, the name of the divine bride: "Prepare an exquisite wedding voyage for your husband. . . .

Mingle your body with that of your husband, and even when you are grey with age you will have the right to speak to the gathered people. . . . Have no evil eye; do not be a husband-killer. Be friendly to animals, good-tempered and glowing with beauty. Bring forth strong sons" (vv. 20, 27, 44)[4].

These two levels of discourse—the narrative and the exhortative, the ancient and the contemporary, the mythical and the real—are clear enough, and clearly separate. They are familiar from other rituals in which the human participants re-enact what was done by the gods. The bride and groom circle the sacred fire together in the Hindu wedding ceremony, as the sun and the moon (Sūryā and Soma) circle together in the sky (v. 18). But between these two levels in this particular hymn there is a third, causal level that joins the human and divine worlds in a series of complex, interlocking ways.

On this third level, the gods (the actors in the ancient story) are brought forward into the present and asked to bless the bride (the actress in the present story). Then there is a subset of verses addressed neither to Sūryā nor to the human bride, nor to the gods who are being asked to bless both of the brides, and these verses imply not merely a parallelism but a direct causal influence of the ancient story upon the present ceremony. One thread of the marriage hymn deals with the problem of defloration, and deals with it on both the narrative and the exhortational levels. Within the ancient narrative, it is said that before being given to Soma, Sūryā was wooed by several other suitors (including the Ashvins, her brothers), and, moreover, that *after* she was given to Soma, she was given to a Gandharva (a kind of fertility spirit) and then to Agni, the god of fire, and then to a mortal: "Soma first possessed her, and the Gandharva possessed her second. Agni was your third husband, and your fourth was the son of a man" (v. 40).

Several different conclusions may be drawn from this line of hand-me-downs, in addition to the obvious implication that Sūryā is a lady who gets around. The verse slips from narrative to exhortation—Sūryā begins as "she" and ends up as "you"—collapsing together the past and the present in the manner that we have already seen. And the line of males ties the past to the present in a similar way. The final male in the series is a mortal; this is a description of the transition from myth to reality, from the time and world of the gods to the time and world of men. But the first two males in the sequence—Soma and the Gandharva—participate both in the world of myth and in the world of reality.

The Gandharva appears earlier in the hymn (vv. 21-22), where he is called by his proper name, Vishvāvasu, and is invoked in the exhortational mode: "'Go away from here! For this woman has a husband.' Thus I implore Vishvāvasu. . . . 'Look for another girl who is ripe and still lives in her father's house. . . . Look for another girl, willing and ready. Leave the wife to unite with the husband.'" Vishvāvasu is a Gandharva; the Gandharvas are demi-gods or demons who preside over sexual union; a "Gandharva marriage" is one consisting of nothing but sexual union, sanctioned by the Gandharvas as the only witnesses. This particular Gandharva, Vishvāvasu, possesses girls before their marriage, exercising a kind of *droit de seigneur*. He is addressed both within the frame of the ancient narrative and within the context of the present ritual: he is asked to leave alone both Sūryā and the contemporary bride.

But in both cases he is asked to go away *only after he has deflowered the bride*. Several verses vividly describe the blood of the defloration of the virgin, blood with a defiling sanctity that has great positive power but is also very dangerous to the bridegroom—unless the first edge of its excessive power has already been absorbed by the obliging Gandharva Vishvāvasu: "The purple and red appears, a magic spirit; the stain is imprinted. . . . Throw away the gown, and distribute wealth to the priests. It becomes a magic spirit walking on feet, and like the wife it draws near the husband. . . . It burns, it bites, and it has claws, as dangerous as poison is to eat. Only the priest who knows the Sūryā hymn is able to receive the bridal gown" (vv. 28-29, 34). The last phrase is particularly significant for our present purposes. "The purple and red" are explicitly referred to in the next verse of this hymn (v. 35) as "the colors of Sūryā, which the priest alone purifies"; that is, the blood of the bride is the blood of Sūryā, of Sūryā deflowered by the Gandharva Vishvāvasu. Nowadays, the gown is no longer used, but the contemporary priest absorbs the ancient power by chanting this very hymn as a kind of magic armor. Thus, the story moves out into the outer frame of contemporary reality, or, if you prefer, the story draws into its inner frame—in 1200 B.C.—the priest, who chants this hymn over the head of a bride who drives to the wedding not in a chariot but on a motorcycle.

And there is another, still more convoluted link that connects the real bride and the mythical groom. The original verse about the transfer of the bride points out that her husband, Soma, had her before the Gandharva Vishvāvasu had her. Soma, too, may avoid the full impact of Sūryā's virginal blood, and it is he who helps the contemporary bridegroom to survive his contact with the blood of the bride. Soma takes the bride first, but he then gives her to the Gandharva, with whom she celebrates the "Gandharva marriage" consisting of sexual union; then she is taken by the god of fire (the very fire that the bride and groom circle in the marriage ritual); and last comes "a son of man," the bridegroom, the descendant of the original "son of man" who married Sūryā *en quatrièmes noces* three thousand years ago. By interposing all of these figures, human and divine, between the initial sacred marriage and the present profane marriage, the myth provides a line of descent, a *paramparā* ("from one to the other") that not only blesses the ceremony with the propitious sanctity of the divine world but draws the sting from the blood of defloration.

The Myth of Married Life

While the Vedic hymn provides a ritual context for contemporary marriages, later Indian mythological texts provide the paradigms that are more frequently looked to by young girls approaching marriage. Generally, Hindu women do not take any of the great Hindu goddesses as their role models, for most of these goddesses—such as the bloodthirsty Kālī—are by definition husbandless; indeed, it is this very lack of a male presence to constrain them that makes them as fierce as they are.[5] Instead, Hindu women look to the wives of the great Hindu Gods—to Pārvatī, the consort of Shiva, and to Sītā, the consort of Rāma. Both of these paradigms are problematic; though each in its way offers an ideal model for human marriage, each also expresses the shadow side of the ideal, the human flaws that inevitably threaten marriage even among the all-too-human gods.

Though Hindu women habitually pray to have a husband "just like Shiva,"[6] there are a number of texts which reveal that these women are also aware of Shiva's serious drawbacks as a husband. Certainly the list of his habits and qualities would strike a Western woman as less than ideal prospects in a husband: Shiva has an on-going commitment to asceticism; he has no money, no house, no job, no clothes; he drugs himself with *bhāng* (marijuana) until he is so stupefied that he cannot even make his rounds as a beggar; and so forth. In Hindu texts, such factors are often cited as criticisms of Shiva not by his wife but rather by her parents;[7] she herself quarrels with him sometimes on this account[8] but more often because of her jealousy of him and her anger at his various adulteries;[9] on one occasion, he even manages to commit adultery with his own wife when she disguises herself, much in the manner of Mozart's *Marriage of Figaro*. But it is also said that Pārvatī loves her husband not in spite of but precisely because of the various factors that her parents cite against him: she is passionately aroused by his unconventional behavior and fascinated by characteristics that seem horrible to those who do not love him (his snakes, his third eye). She is also attracted by his great erotic powers

After nightlong processions, worshippers in Calcutta carry the image of Durgā to the sacred waters of the Hooghly River for immersion.

Opposite top: An idealized female form is typified in this torso from Orissa, which may represent a goddess or a heavenly attendant, *apsara.*

Female Form from Orissa. *14th century. Chlorite, black stone, 8½ x 6½" (22 x 16½ cm). Asutosh Museum of Indian Art, Calcutta.*

Bottom: The divine lovers Krishna and Rādhā.

Alwar School Painting. Rādhā and Krishna. *18th century, miniature. Private collection.*

(Shiva is, after all, the god of the eternally erect phallus), and by the majesty of the god who is regarded by many Hindus as the supreme creator of the universe. Finally, she loves him because he is a god and cannot be judged as normal men are judged.

In Bengal, one of the high points of the ritual year is Durgāpūjā, which celebrates the moment when Durgā (the wife of Shiva, in Bengal) comes back home to visit her family in Bengal but must, at the end of the visit, return to her husband in the Himalayas. Shiva is almost completely excluded from this celebration; magnificent, more-than-life-size images of Durgā are constructed all over the city or village, and offerings are made to her. After days of happy feasting and singing, much of which complains of Shiva's ill-treatment of Durgā, the statues are taken down and carried in procession with torches through the darkness down to the banks of the Ganges. There, with a final burst of drums and chanting and drinking and dancing, the statues of Durgā are cast into the dark waters that will carry her back to the cold mountain cave where her strange husband awaits her.

Rāma, by contrast, is more like a conventional ideal husband: rich, well-born, powerful, handsome, and a paragon of all the Hindu virtues. His wife, Sītā, is the paragon of Hindu wives: beautiful, submissive, loyal, chaste, and steadfast. Sītā was probably once worshipped as an earth goddess in her own right; she is said to have been born out of a furrow of the earth as it was plowed by King Janaka, and many Hindu women still offer her their private homage. But even Sītā's marriage is not always a bed of roses. The Rāmāyana describes how Rāma threw Sītā out, since he feared either that she was actually seduced during her own long exile as the captive of the demon Rāvana, or else that the people of Rāma's kingdom would *think* that Sītā had been seduced. In one version of this story, Sītā goes back in shame and fury to the Earth, her mother, and Rāma never sees her again.[10]

If these marriages made in heaven are something less than perfect, one might perhaps expect Indian women to look to a more romantic model that is freely available to them—Rādhā the beloved of Krishna—in seeking mythical molds into which they might pour their dreams and expectations. And, to a certain extent, Rādhā does supply such a model, though not the same sort of model that Pārvatī and Sītā provide. In the first place, Krishna and Rādhā are not married; the illicit, emotional, even anti-social nature of their love (for in most versions of the myth Rādhā is married to someone else) is the very basis of its sacred quality, in contrast to profane, routine, married love. When reading or hearing the myth of Krishna and Rādhā, therefore, Hindus (both male and female) are reminded *not* to imitate Krishna and Rādhā in any literal way; only the gods can disobey the strict laws that govern the relations between human men and women in India. This is the direct opposite of the logic that operates in the marriage ritual, where humans are taught to do precisely what the gods did.

But there is yet another reason why Krishna and Rādhā do not provide simple role models for husbands and wives: they provide a whole series of possible models, not one ready-made model. In listening to the story of the life of Krishna, or, more often, in watching it as it is performed in the dance-dramas of the Krishna-līlās,[11] each Hindu may take to himself or herself a role selected from any moment of the life cycle and any member of the dramatis personae. That is, a woman may indeed visualize Krishna as a handsome young man, and herself as Rādhā, his mistress; to this extent, Rādhā does provide Hindu women with a focus for many romantic ideas about love, and even about marriage. But a woman may just as well visualize Krishna as a baby, and herself as Yashodā, his mother. Moreover, a *man* may visualize Krishna as a handsome young man and himself as Rādhā; many medieval Bengali saints did just this, dressing in women's clothing and even retiring once a month to menstruate. More precisely, from the Hindu standpoint, one does not *choose* which role to act out in the drama of Krishna; one discovers the role that one *is* acting out, has been acting out, without knowing it.[12] And for a woman, the leading role is not that of Krishna's lover, nor even his wife, but his mother.

Motherhood and Childbirth

The celebration of the birth of a son is the true moment of fulfillment, if not of initiation, of an Indian woman; this is the achievement that justifies her existence and qualifies her as a good human being. Hindu mythology reflects the importance of this moment and also gives a particular form to the natural human emotions that are inherent in the experience of childbirth. As Sudhir Kakar points out, Indians by nature *do* love children, and respect them as separate creatures, not merely as small adults; but the mythology adds yet another dimension to this love by setting it in the context of the worship of the child as god, the infant Krishna.

A major source of the charm and the magic of the cycle of myths about the infant Krishna arises from the interaction between appearance and reality: Krishna *seems* to be an ordinary human child, but in fact he is a god who merely pretends to be a mortal. Throughout his infancy, Krishna accomplishes a series of miracles—killing demons, uprooting giant trees, and so forth—and no one can explain how these acts have been performed, since clearly the babbling baby happily

sucking on his toes nearby had nothing to do with it all, and no one else was present at the scene of the miracle. A double masquerade is taking place here: not only is Vishnu the God pretending to be Krishna the child (one of his incarnations, his eighth *avatār*), but Krishna the son of King Vāsudeva is pretending to be Krishna the son of the cowherd Nanda. The first of these masquerades has approximate parallels in other Indo-European myths: Zeus and Thor wander on earth disguised as mortals, though less often are gods actually *born* as mortals—Jesus is rather a special case. The second masquerade is better known from the pattern of the myth of the birth of the hero: Oedipus, Moses, Romulus and Remus, and many others, including, again, Jesus—the king of heaven who hides in the wilderness or in a humble stable, surrounded by nurturing animals.[13] In the mythology of Krishna, both of these strands combine to present a double halo for the apparently mortal baby: he is both more royal and more divine than he seems to be. The love of the child Krishna is celebrated throughout India in sculpture, painting, song, dance, and every other form of artistic expression; it provides a stage on which mothers can see themselves idealized, but also on which children can see themselves idealized. The fact that Krishna is a particularly *mischievous* child—that he steals butter and throws it to the monkeys, his companions in crime; that, when he grows a little older, he hides the clothes of the girls while they are bathing in the river—is, again, both a cause and a result of the great tolerance with which Indians regard the inevitable pranks of childhood.

But the other, darker side of motherhood and childbirth is also expressed in Indian mythology, and this, too, can be traced all the way back to the Rig Veda. The danger to the unborn embryo is deflected by an incantation that asks Agni to drive away an unnamed evil power, "the one whose name is evil, who lies with disease upon your embryo, your womb, the flesh-eater, the one who kills the embryo as it settles, as it rests, as it stirs, who wishes to kill it when it is born, the one who spreads apart your two thighs, who lies between the married pair, who licks the inside of your womb, the one who bewitches you with sleep or darkness and lies with you. . . ." (Rig Veda 10.162). The danger to the unborn child is then followed by new dangers to the new-born child and the newly delivered mother; the fear of these dangers is expressed in present-day Hinduism in prayers to the goddess Shashtī, the Sixth, so named because she presides over the first six days of the child's life, the critical period. Shashtī is represented as a fair woman with a child in her arms, and her vehicle is a cat; women whose children have died worship her every month, and when a child is six days old, the father worships her. Another sort of mother goddess is Kālī, who rides not on a cat but on a tiger; instead of feeding children, she eats them, and she wears a garland made of the severed heads of children and a belt made of their little hands. Surely Kālī, too, speaks to Indian women of the dangers and terrors of motherhood as eloquently as Pārvatī speaks to them of the dignity and compassion of motherhood.

Krishna's mischievous pranks, such as stealing sweet butter or ghī, are reenacted by this child on Krishna's birthday, *Janmāshtamī*.

Bālā Krishna or baby Krishna shown crawling with sweet laddu in his hand. Such images are used for worship in household shrines.

Bālā Krishna. *19th century. Brass, 3 x 2½ x 1½" (8 x 6½ x 4 cm). Lance Dane Collection at Sanskriti Museum, New Delhi.*

Death and the Embryo

Kālī the Killer is the inevitable shadow aspect of Kālī the Creator of the Universe; death in India is a part of birth and is in its turn a source of birth. The life cycle is truly a *cycle* in India, the end being a new beginning. For this reason, the ancient Vedic funeral ceremony is symbolically structured as a period of gestation and birth; the dead man's soul is an embryo around which the funeral builds a new body by offering balls of rice (representing balls of semen) during ten days that stand for the ten lunar months of pregnancy. The funeral ceremonies are thus directly parallel to the birth ceremonies (*jātakarman*), in which there are also ten days of offerings of food.[14] This symbolic parallelism is explicitly enacted in India, for the person who "feeds" the dead man and builds his new body during the ten days (months) after his death is the man's son, who is thus merely returning the favor that his father did for him ten months before he was born. (This is why it is so important for an Indian man to have a male child: unless a son provides his dead father with the ritual materials with which to construct a new body, the father is doomed to spend the rest of eternity as a ghost in limbo.) The son and father thus give birth to one another in yet another example of the tree-and-seed paradox, even as birth and death themselves give rise to one another.

The embryonic existence of the soul in limbo eventually gives way to a new birth, which may take place in any one of a number of possible wombs. If it is a human womb, the embryo becomes fully conscious during the third month of gestation, a moment which is celebrated with a special quickening ritual. The fact that the embryo is conscious within the womb has certain disadvantages. The story is told of Brihaspati, who tried to rape his pregnant sister-in-law; in the midst of the act, the embryo called out, "Hey, uncle, there isn't room enough for two here, and I was here first." When the embryo's foot actually kicked Brihaspati's semen out of the womb, the frustrated rapist cursed the child to be born blind. (Mahābhārata 1.98.)[15] Moreover, the embryo suffers not only physically (from the discomfort of close confinement in a disgusting mess of blood, pus, and other uterine substances) but mentally: he is tormented by chagrin for his past misdemeanors and anxiety over the anticipated repetitions of his failures. According to the Buddhists, this consciousness (which includes the conscious memory of past lives) is possessed even by the pre-embryonic soul, the soul in limbo, which hovers as a voyeur on the spot where its parents-to-be are copulating: if it loves him and hates her, it becomes born as their daughter; if it hates him and loves her, it becomes born as their son.[16] Thus the child is the witness of every

Jodhpur-Style Painting.
Birth of a Child. *1825. Private Collection.*

196

moment of his life, beginning at a time far before the moment when even the most speculative Freudians place infantile consciousness: the moment *before* conception.

The Child's Eye View of Myth and Life

Children are also the prime witnesses of the mythology which is born from life and gives birth to it. Myth has always been associated with children, though for different reasons at different times: in the ancient world, children were regarded as the pure medium through which mythical ideas became manifest ("out of the mouths of babes"); and even up to the present day in India, myths are the medium through which children first learn much of what their culture needs them to know. At all times, children are the keepers of the mythic vision because they have not yet ineradicably inked in the boundaries in their map of myth and reality; they have not yet learned to point out portions of experience as "not possible" or "not important" or, finally, "not real."[17]

In our culture, children are generally regarded as the only people foolish enough to believe in fairy tales and superheroes (the last survivors in a mythology of atheism); the myth of the incarnate god is reduced to the comic-book tale of Superman disguised as Clark Kent; the shaman's voyage to the gods has become a Star Trek, and the battle between gods and demons a Star War. But the myths are not composed and transmitted by children; they are stories that adults make out of the dreams of childhood. Adults frame the child's view with their own, in a complex series of Chinese boxes: cynical adults tell myths to children, whom they regard as naively gullible, and these myths are about children who experience true mythic realities that are foolishly ignored by the adults in the story. The adult viewing the myth of the child, or watching his own child listen to the myth for the first time, experiences a kind of temporal double-exposure: he feels the event as the first time for the child, and as the second time for himself.[18]

In India, where the world of the child is held in such high esteem, this double standard does not prevail. Children and adults together participate in the rituals of life and listen to the telling of the tales; mothers bring their children with them when they go to the temples to hear the stories of the gods told by the temple priests. Indeed, children may be the key to the preservation of the world of myth in India as well as in America. For India, too, is under pressure from the rationalists and modernizers to demythologize. True, Krishna-līlās and Rām-līlās are still celebrated even in many highly urbanized settings,

Kālī, the destroyer of evil, is shown with a garland of the heads and arms of her enemies and with her hands dripping blood.

197

Modern comic-book version of Durgā killing the buffalo demon Mahishāsura.

and people still travel from the cities to the country to see performances in their traditional settings. And the myths survive in modern avatārs: lurid Hindi films depict the battles of gods and demons, and the Indian version of our own Classic Comics—the Amar Chitra Kathā ("Immortal Picture Stories")—presents the ancient classics in a strangely Westernized but still recognizably Indian form.

But as people move from the villages to the cities, the professional storytellers—those who present the dance dramas of the myths or recite the long epics, in Sanskrit or in the vernacular of the district— lose part of their audience. And even more important than the possibility that the particular craft of the storytellers may die out is the undeniable fact that, already, the *setting* for storytelling is fast dying out—the occasions when stories are told, the moments of quiet work at the loom or on the threshing floor, the long winter evenings around the fire. But children again are a safeguard against this loss; for however busy one may be, working in a factory or at an office desk, there still comes a moment when food is prepared and eaten, when children are washed and made ready for bed. And there, as here, a small voice will say, "Tell me a story."

To the rhythm of everyday
chores, such as grinding
flour, mothers often sing
stories to their children.

The Child in India
Sudhir Kakar

Within the wide diversity of India, its welter of distinct regional, linguistic, caste, and religious groupings, there is still a unified cultural awareness of the child that informs the behavior of parents and other adult caretakers. This cultural awareness, a specific Indian conception of the nature of children and the place of childhood in the life cycle, derives from many sources. There are passages dealing with children in the law books of the Hindus, while the section on the care and upbringing of the children, the *Bālānga*, is an integral part of traditional Indian medicine, *Ayurveda*. There are references to children and childhood in such ancient epics as the Rāmāyana and Mahābhārata and descriptions of childhood in classical Sanskrit and medieval vernacular literature. In addition, the symbolic content of the various rites of childhood, and of the traditional folk songs that accompany them, provide some indications as to what Indians consider the chief characteristic of a given stage of childhood. While much of this material may seem to belong to the literate traditions of the Hindu upper castes, anthropological accounts have shown that such traditions are basically much the same in many lower groups, their continuous and continuing survival in large sections of society being one of the most distinctive features of the Indian culture.[1]

Ideology of Childhood

The first theme that stands out in the Indian cultural traditions is the intense parental longing for children, especially sons who can carry on the family line. This is important because of the emphasis placed on celibacy by the Buddhists and the Jains. A number of myths and didactic passages in the epics repeatedly emphasize that begetting a son is one of man's highest duties and the only way he can discharge the debt he owes to his ancestors. Consider the story of Jaratkuru.

> The renowned ascetic Jaratkuru, full of merit and great spiritual power derived from his sustained asceticism, was wandering around the world when one day he came across a deep pit. In this pit, the spirits of his ancestors—the *pitris*—were hanging head down, their feet tied to a tree trunk by a single skein of rope that was gradually being nibbled away by a large rat. It was evident that the pitris would soon fall down into the deep darkness of the pit. Moved by their pitiable condition, Jaratkuru enquired whether he could somehow save them from this fate, expressing his readiness to do so even if he had to give up

Within the sacred precincts of the temple, a Hindu boy learns the traditions of his forefathers.

all rewards to which his great asceticism entitled him. "Venerable ascetic," the spirits of his ancestors answered, "thou desirest to relieve us! . . . O child, whether it is asceticism or sacrifice or whatever else there be of very holy acts, everything is inferior. These cannot count equal to a son. O child, having seen all, speak unto Jaratkuru of ascetic wealth . . . tell him all that would induce him to take a wife and beget children![2]

Another ascetic, Mandapala, is told in no uncertain terms that in spite of his most ascetic efforts, certain celestial regions will forever remain closed to him, for they can be reached only by those who have had children: "'Beget children therefore!' Mandapala is instructed, 'Thou shalt then enjoy multifarious regions of felicity!'"[3] Children in the Mahābhārata are not only seen as instrumental in the fulfillment of a sacred duty which, however agreeable and meritorious, still carries the connotation of religious necessity and social imposition. They are also portrayed as a source of emotional and sensual gratification. Listen to Shakuntalā, the forsaken wife of Dushyanta, asking the king to acknowledge his son:

By sounding the sacred conch shell trumpet, evil influences and spirits are dispelled and the protective gods and goddesses are called to the altar to receive their offerings. At the birth of a child conch shell trumpets are blown to dispel evil and call the beneficial deities to protect the newborn.

A proud father carrying his new child. The black dot on the forehead is to avert the evil eye.

What happiness is greater than what the father feels when the son is running towards him, even though his body is covered with dust, and clasps his limbs? Even ants support their own without destroying them, then why shouldst not thou, virtuous as thou art, support thy own child? The touch of soft sandal paste of women, of (cool) water is not so agreeable as the touch of one's own infant son locked in one's embrace. As a Brāhman is the foremost of all bipeds, a cow, the foremost of all quadrupeds, a guru, the foremost of all superiors, so is the son the foremost of all objects agreeable to touch. Let, therefore, this handsome child touch thee in embrace. There is nothing in the world more agreeable to the touch than the embrace of one's son.

Sanskrit poets, too, have waxed lyrical over the parental longing for children and the parents' emotions at the birth of a child. In two well-known examples, Bhavabhūti describes Rāma's love for Lava and Kusha, while Bānabhatta rhapsodizes over Prabhakarvardhana's love for his son, Harsha. The greatest of all Sanskrit poets, Kālidāsa, in his *Raghuvamsha*, describes Dilīpa's response to Raghu's birth thus:

He went in immediately (on hearing the news) and as the lotus becomes motionless when the breeze stops, he gazed at his son's face with the same still eyes. Just as tides come into the ocean when it sees the moon, similarly the King (Dilīpa) was so happy on seeing his son that he could not contain the happiness in his heart.[4]

The demands of objectivity compel us to report that the intense parental longing and pleasure at the birth of a child in the Indian tradition is generally limited to sons. Girls receive a more muted reception. Although a first-born daughter may be regarded by parents as a harbinger of good luck, the welcome accorded to further daughters declines markedly.

Contemporary anthropological studies from different parts of India and the available clinical evidence assure us that the traditional preference for sons is very much intact.[5] At the birth of the son drums are beaten in some parts of the country, conch shells are blown in others, and the midwife is paid lavishly, but no such spontaneous rejoicing accompanies the birth of a daughter. Women's folk songs reveal a painful awareness of their ascribed inferiority—of this discrepancy, at birth, between the celebration of sons and the mere tolerance of daughters. Thus, in a north Indian song, the women complain:

'Listen, O Sukhmā, what a tradition has started!
Drums are played upon the birth of a boy,
But at my birth only a brass plate was beaten'.[6]

And in Maharashtra, the girl, comparing herself to a white sweet-scented jasmin (*jai*) and the boy to the big, strong-smelling flower (*keorā*), plaintively asks:

> *Did anyone notice the sweet fragrance of a jai?* The hefty keorā however has filled the whole street with its strong scent'.[7]

The second major element in the Indian ideology of the child is the great emphasis placed on protective indulgence, as compared to the element of "disciplining the child" which has been prominent in much of the Western history of childhood. In the law books, children belong to a group consisting of women, the aged, the sick, and the infirm—those who deserve society's protection and claim its indulgence. Thus, even before serving invited guests (and guests as we know are almost on a par with gods in the Indian tradition), the householder is enjoined to feed pregnant women, the sick, and the young.[8] Although a man may not quarrel with learned men, priests, or teachers, he is also forbidden to speak harshly to the aged, the sick, or children.[9] Whereas the king is within his rights to exact retribution from those who question his authority or inveigh against his person, he is required to forgive children (as also the old and the sick) who may be guilty of lese majesty. Although punishments, including fines, are prescribed for everyone soiling the king's highways, children are specifically exempted; they are only to be reprimanded and are required to clean up after themselves.[10]

The protective indulgence shown toward the child is manifested most clearly where it matters the most (at least to the child), namely, in the pronouncements in the law books of the Hindus on the chastisement of children. Children are only to be beaten with a rope or a bamboo stick split at the end. The split bamboo, as we may remember from circus clowns' mock fights, makes a loud noise without inflicting much pain. Moreover, even this punishment is to be carried out only on the back and never on a "noble part," i.e., not on the head or chest. To those who hold progressive views on child discipline, the beating of children may hardly seem like "protective indulgence." However, the extent of this indulgence becomes strikingly clear when we compare Indian law books with the legal texts of other ancient societies. For example, there is evidence in the law codes and digests of ancient Rome to suggest that brutal forms of child abuse were common; it was only as late as A.D. 374 that infanticide was declared a capital offense in the Roman world.[12]

The humane attitude toward the child in India is also apparent in the medical texts which contain detailed and copious instructions on the care of the young child. These wide-ranging instructions on such diverse topics as the time when a child should be encouraged to sit up and the specification of toys with regard to color, size, and shape reflect great solicitude concerning the period of infancy and early childhood. The voices of ancient doctors sound strangely modern as they expound on the relationship between child-rearing practices and personality development. For example, the practice of persuading the child to eat or to stop crying by conjuring up threatening visions of ghosts, goblins, and ferocious animals, they tell us, is to be avoided because it has a very harmful effect.[13] The child should not be awakened from sleep suddenly, they go on to say, nor should he be snatched or thrown up in the air. He should not be irritated, and he should be kept happy at all costs, as this is crucial for his psychological development and future well-being.[14] With compassion and tenderness for the young, the texts strive to develop the adult caretaker's capacity to comprehend the needs and emotions of the child—needs that are apt to be overlooked since they are articulated in voices that are frail and words that are indistinct.

Besides the longing and protective indulgence, the third element in the Indian ideology is a celebration, even an idealization of the child and childhood. In the most powerful surviving literary tradition of northern and central India, for instance, such poets of the *bhakti* movement as Sūrdās and Tulsīdās have placed childhood close to the center of poetic consciousness and creativity. Sūrdās, in fact, composed five hundred verses on Krishna's childhood alone![15] Indeed, in this poetry the celebration of the Divine takes place through the metaphor of celebration of the child. The aspects that are admiringly emphasized as divine attributes are the child's freedom and spontaneity, his simplicity, charm, and delight in self.

Krishna is singing in the courtyard.
He dances on his small feet, joyous within.
Lifting up his arms, he shouts for the black
    and white cows.
Sometimes he calls Nandbābā, sometimes he goes in and out of
    the house.
Seeing his reflection, he tries to feed it.
Hidden, Yashodā watches the play that makes her so happy.

Sūrdās says, to see Krishna's play everyday is bliss.[16]

Tulsīdās sings:

Self-willed he (Rāma) insists on having the moon.
He sees his shadow and is frightened.
Clapping his hands, he dances.
Seeing his child-play

To indulge a child, even the impossible is not refused. Here Rāma, in this miniature painting, is given the moon, reflected in a dish.
National Museum, New Delhi.

All mother-hearts are brimming over with happiness.
Becoming angry, he is obstinate.
And remains stubborn till he gets what he wants.

Tulsīdās says, the sons of the King of Ayodhyā live in the temple of his heart.[17]

In an adult-centered world that overvalues abstractions, prudence, and reason, it is refreshing to find popular Indian poetry celebrating such childlike virtues as intensity and vivaciousness, capacity for sorrow and delight, mercurial anger and an equally quick readiness to forgive and forget injuries. In the Indian vision, these qualities are not seen as "childish," to be socialized out of existence, but valuable attributes of humans—of all ages—since they are an expression of the Divine.

Traditions of Childhood: Western and Indian

In Western antiquity, until perhaps the thirteenth century, adult attitudes towards children were generally dominated by an ideology that had little empathy for the needs of children.[18] This ideology looked upon the child as a nuisance and an unwanted burden, perfunctorily tolerating brutal treatment of children by their parents as well as such associated phenomena as infanticide, the sale of children, and their casual abandonment. It is also demonstrable, however, that there has been a gradual progression in the Western ideology of the child. From the earlier external suppression that permitted physical torture, by the sixteenth and seventeenth centuries the ideological emphasis was decisively shifting towards an internal suppression in which child training and discipline were stressed.

From parental efforts aimed at conquering the child's will, the Western ideology of caretaking progressed further in the nineteenth and twentieth centuries, when the awareness of the sensibilities and needs of children increased appreciably. This movement towards the fostering attitude continues unabated.

The conflict between the rejecting and nurturing attitude towards the child, so marked in the Western history of childhood, is, then, absent in the Indian tradition. As we have seen, the evidence from disparate sources—from medicine to literature, from law to folk songs—is overwhelming that the child in Indian tradition is ideologically considered a valuable and welcome human being to whom the adults are expected to afford their fullest protection, affection, and indulgence. Consider the reflection of this ideology in linguistic usage. In Hindi, for example, what adults do to children is *pālnā poshnā*—protecting-nurturing. They are not "trained," "reared," or "brought up." With its implications of training the child, teaching him to conform to social norms, and "channeling his impulses," the model of *socialization* (which governs contemporary Western caretaking) was a logical next step in a historical evolution from the preceding model of disciplining and conquering a child's will. In its general orientation and focus, such a model is necessarily foreign to the Indian consciousness. In fact, as we saw in our short discussion of *bhakti* songs and poems, the Indian tradition of childhood values precisely those attributes of the child which have *not* been "socialized." Here it is the child who is considered nearest to a perfect, divine state, and it is the adult who needs to learn the child's mode of experiencing the world. This is not to suggest, however, that the norms and values of adulthood are not conveyed to the child; as we shall see, they are imparted through a clear set of expectations and in a manner that is highly ritualized.

Stages of Indian Childhood

The notion of the human life cycle unfolding in a series of stages, with each stage having its unique "tasks" and moral responsibilities, is an established part of traditional Indian thought, best exemplified in the well-known scheme of *āshrama-dharma*. The four *āshrams* or life stages—student, householder, recluse, and renouncer—as elaborated in the texts, however, focus largely on the period of youth and adulthood and neglect to assign any formal importance to the stages of childhood. We must then turn to the popular understanding of the childhood stages as they are lived in the villages and towns of India and to the rites, the samskāras—the expressive and symbolic performances and ceremonies that focus on the child and mark his transition from one stage to another. An understanding of these stages and the rites marking them is essential to increase our appreciation of the artifacts, objects, and performances to which they have given birth.

The rites of childhood have twin goals. First, they seek to refine and transform the innate nature of the child at birth. Second, the rites aim at a gradual integration of the child into society. The samskāras, in other words, beat time to measured movement that takes the child away from the original mother-infant symbiosis into a full-fledged

With rattle in hand, this young girl learns to care for a tiny infant while her mother works nearby.

membership of his community. In different parts of Hindu India and even within the same village there may be variations in the way these rites are performed.[19] Variations within a particular village may be partly due to differences in caste, with the higher castes celebrating more life cycle rites, and partly due to differences in wealth, which determines whether individual rites may be performed on separate occasions or several rites must be combined on one occasion.

The First Stage: Garbha

Since life in Indian thought is presumed to begin with conception, the first stage of the life cycle is *garbha*, the fetal period, and the first rite is *garbhadāna*. It is held immediately after marriage, which provides the appropriate context for conception. The rite is considered obligatory for all householders and highlights the parental wish for offspring, the chief goal of an Indian marriage. The rite also "reminds" the parents and the community of the momentous nature of conception when the soul's "subtle body" enters the conceptus at the moment of fertilization. The qualities of the sperm, the ovum, the *rasa* ("organic sap" or "nutrition"), and the psychic constellation of the soul from its previous incarnation are considered to be the determinants of the embryo's functional and structural growth.

The critical period of fetal development is said to begin in the third month, when the latent "mind" of the fetus becomes conscious or *chetan*. In this stage of *dauhridaya* (literally "bi-cardiac," with one heart belonging to the fetus and the other to the mother), the unborn child and the mother function psychologically as a unit, mutually influencing each other. The feelings and affects of the fetus—a legacy from its previous birth—are transmitted to the mother through the channels of nutrition. For the future psychological well-being of the child it is imperative that the cravings of the pregnant woman be fully gratified (since they are those of the unborn child) and the unit of pregnant mother and fetus be completely indulged.

The rite marking this period is *godha-bharāna*, which honors the expectant mother. The expectant mother is dressed in a new sari, presented glass bangles, and fed culturally valued foods by the "superior" members of the household, thus reversing the usual order of eating and service. In many parts of the country, this rite is a family affair which does not require an officiating priest. In others, the rite may be accompanied by feasts arranged in gardens outside the house, with much singing of traditional songs, the *sohara*. These both celebrate the occasion and instruct the expectant mother in such matters as the dietary restrictions she must observe during her pregnancy.

The Second Stage: Shishu

Birth begins the second stage of the Indian life cycle of infancy or the *shishu* period, which extends for the first three to four years of the child's life. During this period of prolonged infancy, the Indian child is intensely and intimately attached to his mother. This attachment is an exclusive one, not in the sense of the child being without older and younger siblings close in age who claim, and compete for, the mother's love and care, but in that the Indian child up to the age of four or five directs his demands exclusively toward his mother. This is so in spite of the customary presence in the extended family of many other potential caretakers and substitute mothers. Constantly held, cuddled, crooned and talked to, the Indian infant's experience of his mother is a heady one; his contact with her is of an intensity and duration that differentiate it markedly from the experience of infancy in Western cultures. At the slightest whimper or sign of distress, the infant is picked up and rocked, or given the breast and comforted. Usually, it is the infant's own mother who swiftly moves to pacify him, although in her occasional absence on household matters it may be a sister or an aunt or a grandmother who takes up to feed or clean or just soothe

Even as she carefully paints a border design this artist keeps her infant cuddled safely on her lap.

him with familiar physical contact. It is by no means uncommon to see an old grandmother pick up a crying child and give him her dried-up breast to suck as she sits there, rocking on her heels and crooning over him.

From the moment of birth, then, and in consonance with the Indian ideology of the child, the infant is greeted and surrounded by direct, sensual body contact, by relentless physical ministrations.[20] An Indian mother is inclined towards total indulgence of her infant's wishes and demands, whether these be related to feeding, cleaning, sleeping, or being kept company. Moreover, she tends to extend this kind of mothering well beyond the time when the "infant" is ready for independent functioning in many areas. Thus, for example, feeding is frequent, at all times of the day and night, and "on demand." And although breast feeding is supplemented with other kinds of food after the first year, the mother continues to give her breast to her child for as long as possible, often up to two or three years: in fact, suckling comes to a gradual end only when there is a strong reason to stop nursing, such as a second pregnancy. And breast contact between mother and infant, we know, is not only conducive to the child's psychological development but is a safeguard against infant mortality.

Similarly without any push from the family, the Indian toddler takes his own time learning to control his bowels, and proceeds at his own pace to master such skills as walking, talking, and dressing himself. As far as the mother's and family's means permit, an infant's wishes are fully gratified and his unfolding capacities and activities accepted, if not always with manifest delight, at least with affectionate tolerance.

The rites that mark this period of infancy are designed to gradually separate the child from the mother and prepare his entry into the wider world of the community. First, there is the *jātakarma* rite, performed just after delivery of the offspring. After the new-born is cleaned, the father comes in to look at the baby's face. The paternal act of looking at a first-born son, the sacred texts assure him, will absolve him of all his debts to the gods and to his ancestors. The birth of a girl is slightly less meritorious; her gift in marriage brings the father spiritual merit and appreciably increases the store of his good *karma*. Having seen the infant's face, the father goes out and takes a ritual bath. Accompanied by the priests and family elders the father then re-enters the maternity room for the birth ceremonies. He prays for the growth of the infant's talent and intellect, thanks the spot of earth where the birth took place, and praises and thanks the mother for bearing a strong child.

The next samskāra is the naming rite of *nāmakarna*. Depending upon the mother's condition and the auspiciousness of the astrological constellations, this may happen on the tenth, twelfth, fifteenth, or thirty-second postpartum day. The mother and infant emerge from the seclusion of the maternity room into the bustle of an expectant family, as the mother ceremoniously places the baby in the father's lap for the name-giving ceremony.

From the family, the mother and infant unit moves into the wider world in the third or fourth month with the performance of *nishakrāmana*, the child's first outing or "looking at the sun" and "looking at the moon," as the texts poetically describe the infant's ritual introduction to the world and the cosmos. Between the sixth and ninth months, the important rite of *annaprāshana* marks the first time the child is given solid food and thus the onset of a gradual weaning and its psychological counterpart—the process of the child's separation from his mother. In this rite, after prayers to the goddess, a priest offers oblations to the infant's ancestors in his name, thus, in a sense, formally connecting the infant to past generations. Relatives and family friends in the village present the infant with gifts, which minimally include a set of eating utensils—a plate, a bowl, a glass, and perhaps a wooden seat.

Elaborate *kolam* designs are prepared in the temple to protect and cleanse the area of worship.

The Third Stage: Bālā

If the rites are any guide, the period of infancy is deemed complete by the third year, to be followed by the *bālā* or early childhood stage. Whereas previous rites were common for both male and female infants, now the life cycles of boys and girls begin to diverge. For most females, there are no further rites of childhood; the next principal samskāra in their life cycle will be that of marriage.

For a boy, the early childhood begins with the important rite of *mundan* or tonsure. The child is generally taken to the temple of a mother goddess (to the bank of a river in some regions), where his baby hair is shaved and offered to the goddess. In other regions, mundan may be a purely family affair. He is dressed up in new clothes which are miniature replicas of those worn by adult members of his community. The symbolism of death and rebirth—psychologically the death of the mother-infant symbiosis and the birth of the child as a separate individual—is at the heart of the many rituals connected with mundan. Accordingly, in the Bhojpuri region of northern India, before the child's head is shaved and he is dressed in new clothes, the women of the family take the child to the Ganges and ceremoniously cross the river in a boat.[21] The symbolism of crossing the river, of death and rebirth, is apparent. Moreover, the folk songs sung at the time of mundan are the sohars, the songs that are also sung at birth. In the popular tradition, it is only after the child's tonsure that he is considered ready for the process of discipline and the family's efforts at socialization.

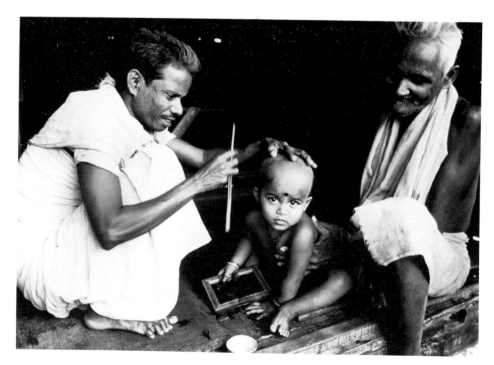

A child is given his first haircut on an auspicious day and generally during special temple festivals.

The Fourth Stage: Kumāra

It is only in the stage of late childhood, *kumāra*, which begins around the age of five to seven years, that the cultural expectations and experiences of boys and girls begin to diverge markedly. For the boy, the world of childhood widens from the intimate cocoon of maternal protection to the unfamiliar masculine network woven by the demands and tensions, the comings and goings, of the men of the family. The most striking feature of his experience is the contrast between an earlier, more or less unchecked benevolent indulgence and the new inflexible standards. As an anthropological account of a Hyderabad village describes the male child's "second birth": "The liberty that he was allowed during this early childhood is increasingly curtailed. Now the accent is on good behavior and regular habits."[22] And a north Indian proverb, with counterparts in other regions of the country, pithily conveys what the boy has to now face: "Treat a son like a *rāja* for the first five years, like a slave for the next ten, and like a friend thereafter."

By contrast; the Indian daughter is not severed from the other women in the household, although she is given new, "grown up" household tasks and responsibilities, especially in the care of younger children in the family. Her childhood, as compared to her brother's, is shortened in the sense that she takes on domestic responsibilities at an age when her brother is still playing on the streets or, at the most, running small errands.

The difference does not persist in tasks related to the family's occupation. Both boys and girls are initiated at the age of nine or ten into craft skills which they master by the age of fifteen or sixteen, an age at which the children of the farming community are just beginning to be seriously involved in their occupation. In both groups, however, the world of children is not isolated from that of adults, as it is in modern technological societies. Even very young children share the craft or agricultural environment of the adults. An arresting glimpse from a study of children in communities of craftsmen reveals: "When a four-year-old girl in a potters' group cried for her mother's attention, and the mother was ill with fever, the father took her over and distracted her with clay, telling her gently that she should do what he was doing with the ball of clay. Similarly, the young mothers continue their spinning or cutting or block printing with the children around them; sometimes the children go to sleep at the work spot."[23] The child as an inheritor of traditional craft skills is integrated into the family quite differently from a child whose social order emphasizes freedom of opportunity to choose his work, even if the freedom is

Wheels on sticks amuse these potential truck drivers who play while their sister washes pots and pans.

functionally a limited one and sometimes degenerates into his exploitation as a cheap source of labor.

Discipline in the stage of late childhood becomes a serious affair, with scolding and occasionally light spanking being the main disciplining techniques. Children are rarely praised *openly* for performing assigned tasks or fulfilling adult expectations. This lack of praise does not derive from an absence of parental pride, but rather from the belief that open admiration and praise is risky, since it may well attract the evil eye or otherwise tempt the fates. As numerous studies of Indian childhood have shown, child battering is an extremely rare phenomenon even in the poorest and most deprived groups of society, such as the slums of Bombay.[24] There may be cases of neglect of children, especially in the areas of health care and nutrition, but almost never gross physical abuse. Nothing else can so clearly highlight the continuing strength of the traditional Indian ideology in influencing the contemporary reality of childhood.

Throughout this period, the child is exposed to a whole range of activities which have had as their goal the education of the child into the culture of his birth. Stories of great heroes drawn from the Rāmāyana and Mahābhārata and the Purānas are told, usually by the grandparents, to inculcate virtues the culture regards as praiseworthy. Worldly wisdom is taught through folk tales and the animal stories from the *Panchātāntra*. Festivals, fairs, community congregations, bardic songs, pilgrimages, folk dances and music, visiting theatrical troupes, and wandering sāddhus all introduce the child to the larger gamut of life surrounding him, as well as mold his aesthetic sensibilities in a culturally desired fashion.

The rites of this period of childhood, mostly limited to boys of the upper castes, are *vidyārambha* and the *upanayana*. Vidyārambha, performed between the fifth and seventh years, when the child is supposed to be old enough to learn to read and write, is an initiation into learning. Upanayana, on the other hand, marks the culmination, the grand end of childhood. Traditionally performed (depending upon the caste) anywhere between the eighth and twelfth years, upanayana initiates the child's "social birth" into the wider community. As a text puts it, "Till a boy is eight years old he is like one newly born, and only indicates the caste in which he is born. As long as his upanayana ceremony has not been performed the boy incurs no blame as to what is allowed or forbidden!"[25] The initiation ceremony is elaborate, its preparatory rites designed to drive home the fact of the child's separation from his family and the final break with his mother. In its traditional version, the child is smeared with a yellowish paste and expected to spend the whole night in a pitch-dark room in absolute silence—a re-creation of the embryonic state—before he emerges the next morning for one of the most moving and poignant ceremonies of this samskāra, the sharing of a meal with his mother, which is supposedly the last time the mother and son will ever eat together. Thus, although as an initiation rite, upanayana contains many rituals symbolizing a hopeful beginning, it nevertheless also clearly marks the regretted end of a familiar world—the world of childhood.

Under the careful scrutiny
of his elders a young balladeer from Rajasthan learns
the techniques of painting
the parh scroll.

Performance, Music and the Child

Nazir A. Jairazbhoy

> In places in which there occur instrumental music and dramatic performance, or song and instrumental music, there will surely be there never any kind of inauspicious happening. (*Nātyashāstra* XXXVI:28)

The word "performance" has many meanings and implications. To most Western readers it will bring to mind the theatrical stage—a play, an opera, or a concert. These events are indeed performances. But the word performance is now frequently used to refer to a broad scope of human activities or actions among which stage presentations are just one of the many types. In the context of music, for instance, the term performance could apply equally to a mother who sings a lullaby to her child, devotees singing devotional songs, *bhajan*, in a temple, or a shaman producing obscure unintelligible utterances addressed to a deity, not to mention all the forms of expression directed to human audiences and thus qualifying as performance in the conventional sense of the term. In his *Essays in Performance Theory 1970-1976*, Richard Schechner observes:

> Performance is a very inclusive notion of action: theatre is only one node on a continuum that reaches from ritualization in animal behavior (including humans) through performances in everyday life—greetings, displays of emotion, family scenes and so on—to rites, ceremonies and performances: large-scale theatrical events.

In India, children are witnesses to, as well as subjects of, this wide variety of performance types virtually from the moment they are born; in fact, they are addressed during ritual performances prior to birth and even before conception. From birth, they witness rituals, plays, and actions of all kinds, for children in India are typically an integral part of all but the most formal urban Western performance genres (i.e., the concerts of Western music presented frequently in such cosmopolitan cities as Bombay, Calcutta, Delhi, and Madras). It is not uncommon to find children and even babies attending concerts of urban Indian classical music in the cities of India, or peeking at adult performance events through the cracks of doors and windows left casually ajar. On other occasions a mother may sing and play a drum in a ritual village performance, such as those of the Dholī community in the state of Rajasthan, with her infant seated on her lap.

Not only are children witnesses to all manner of performances, but some are even performers themselves, since apprenticeship into the world of adults begins at a tender age in many spheres of Indian life.

Opposite: With an oversized drum (*dholak*) and a handy tin can these budding percussionists playfully strike up a traditional dance rhythm.

Walking alone through a field of wheat and flowering mustard, a mendicant-bard sings a religious ballad to the accompaniment of a small tambourine.

As in other cultures, children perform copiously among themselves, adding an extra dimension to the performance experience of the child, one which Indian adults have lived through and recall frequently in their nostalgic moments.

Many performers in India gear their acts to the world of children, not only to amuse and entertain them but also to cure and bless them, in the process introducing them to traditional values and customs and helping to shape the aesthetic responses which will influence them for the rest of their lives. Particularly in rural India, adults tend to preserve and cherish some of the child-like qualities of innocence and wonderment which enable them to empathize readily with the world of the child and to relive the magic moments of their own childhood experiences through performances. Many performers instinctively grasp this child-adult ambivalence and cater to it in special ways. While relating a serious historical narrative, for instance, a string puppeteer will periodically introduce lighter moments, such as a little skit about a puppet toy-drummer who keeps interrupting the narrative by his off-rhythm drumming, or a puppet who not only juggles a ball from hand to hand but also balances it on his shoulder, head, and other parts of his body. In India, children and adults sitting together in the audience would likely share the hilarity of the toy-drummer and respond to the juggling puppet with similar amazement and disbelief.

The nature of the involvement of the Indian child in performance and music is a function of both the unique interrelationship which exists between ritual and other types of performance in India, and the static/dynamic elements of tradition and modernity which at present confront India as well as other Third World countries.

The origins of ritual appear to be rooted in the idea that when performances (i.e., actions) succeed, whether in empirical or psychological terms, they are likely to be repeated again and again until they acquire a ritual status. As the community begins to believe that the

Above: Flying leaps and twitching shoulders, sensuous rhythms and rude language are all essential ingredients of the *bhangra*, a traditional farmers' dance from the Punjab.

reenactment of a performance with a considerable measure of accuracy is necessary for success, the action becomes a formalized, ritualized performance, with only little innovation being tolerated. Schechner explains that the Western view of a performance as something "make believe," "in a play," "for fun," and "fundamentally experimental," is less meaningful in a society such as India's, which is noted for the depth and longevity of its ritual-related performing traditions. This is not to suggest that there is absolutely no room for improvisation or experimentation in a traditional performance in India, but rather that this kind of formalized performance can hardly be described as being "fundamentally experimental." Viewed over long periods of time, however, all traditions can be seen as being in a continual state of flux, some in the process of generation and others in degeneration, even though they may appear superficially to be stable.

In India today, as in so many other Asian countries, many age-old traditions are in the process of breaking down, with ritual acts being simplified or, in some instances, being abandoned completely. For many performers it is also a time of discovery, of improvisation and experimentation, as they find that the successful actions which have been preserved as ritual and ceremony in the past are increasingly less meaningful today. Performers are thus being obliged to redefine the actions that will lead to success in modern India. While change—

In the open air of the nomad camp, Kalbelia women perform a lively folk dance accompanied by their menfolk.

Right: A court performer combines juggling and dance to entertain a nobleman and his retainers.

Pahāri School. Woman Juggling. *18th century. Painting on paper, 8¾ x 11" (23 x 29 cm). National Museum, New Delhi.*

sometimes even violent change—has always existed in all communities, most societies manage to preserve continuity with their past. One of the ways they have accomplished this has been through the handing down of traditions, rituals, and ceremonies through both written and, especially in countries such as India, oral sources. In fact, these oral repositories have been the real archives and museums of traditional societies—the human carriers of *knowledge of the ways of doing*, not just their perishable products housed within four walls. Often, the handing over of this traditional knowledge to the younger generation is symbolized by a ritual. In a boy's *upanayana* ceremony, he is given a triple thread to wear across his body that represents his tie to the ancient civilization of the Indo-Aryans and acknowledges his indebtedness to his father, ancient seers, and gods. The informal transmission of knowledge to children is, however, equally as important. From the earliest moments of awareness, when a child observes the oldest generation of practitioners, he receives a thread from the previous century.

Ancient Classical Theater

In India, formalized performance undoubtedly dates back to the pre-Aryan period, but little is known about performance from that era. The rituals of Vedic Aryan society, which probably go back three thousand or more years, have, however, been preserved in great detail; they provide the perfect illustration of the power of oral tradition serving as a community "archives" by preserving knowledge of the way of performing these ancient rituals, including the knowledge of how to make the artifacts necessary for the performance. These include special implements and shaped bricks for altars, earthen vessels, as well as ancient techniques for making fires. There is no concrete evidence of any other formal performance tradition with this kind of longevity in India.

In his *Astādhyāyī*, the grammarian Pānini (c. fifth century B.C.) incidentally refers to a work entitled *Natasūtra* (aphoristic rules for the *nata*, usually translated as actor, dancer, or mime) which is, unfortunately, not extant, but its title is highly suggestive, since several groups of performers in present-day India claim to belong to the community of Nat. There is undoubtedly some connection between the two, but the precise nature of the connection is open to conjecture.

The earliest extensive source of information on performance in ancient India which still survives today is the Nātyashāstra, a treatise dated variously by scholars from the second century B.C. to fifth century A.D., which describes a particular dramatic tradition, *nātya*, incorporating music and dance. The performances must have involved

Graceful dancers and musicians carved in stone at Konarak, inspired 19th-century dancers to revive the classical dance of the early medieval period—11th century.

a large cast of actors as well as musicians, dancers, and stage hands. The most striking feature of this ancient dramatic tradition was in the way it attempted to integrate all the performing arts with the crafts and sciences of that time. Bhārata, the author of the Nātyashāstra states, "There is no wise maxim, no learning, no art or craft, no device, no action which is not found in the drama (nātya). Hence I have devised the drama in which meet all the departments of knowledge, different arts and various actions."

This dramatic tradition evidently continued in India for about a thousand years, culminating in what is commonly referred to as classical Sanskrit theater with the plays of Kālidāsa, Bāna, and others. Then it gradually faded away, perhaps because of the Muslim conquests from the north and west. Some of the existing dramatic traditions show many elements of continuity with early nātya.

Although the Nātyashāstra provides information on just one type of ancient performance, it would be safe to deduce that there were probably many others existing at that time, perhaps more modest in scope, but equally, if not more, meaningful to society at large. Among these must have been the bards and storytellers/singers who created and transmitted the epics Mahābhārata and Rāmāyana and the Purānic stories, whose texts were only later committed to writing. In addition, ancient India must have had folk songs and dances to commemorate festive occasions and life and agricultural cycle rites as well as a variety of work-related activities, all of which are common throughout India today. Unfortunately, the performance aspects of these are not described in any of the early literature, although there are occasional tantalizing hints.

Varieties of
Performance in India Today

In many respects, India is more like a continent than a country, for it encompasses a great variety of ethnic and racial groups, languages, and customs. Performance styles reflect this huge diversity, not only regionally, but also in terms of the different communities of performers, genres being performed, the environments in which the performances take place, and other factors.

Broadly speaking, performances can be divided into three levels of activities: home events, community events, and public events. In actuality, these areas often overlap and performance tends to evolve from one to another over a period of time. The Indian child first experiences the events of the home, including the family outings to the temple or town, and is gradually exposed to those of the local community and, finally, the wider public. Most often, such forays into the outer world are made in the context of a performance: ritual, social, musical, dramatic, or a combination of these.

Home performance events involve the family unit and are basically private in nature, although they are often presided over by a priest or some other specialist performer. These home events frequently overlap into the community on such important occasions as weddings, the birth of a male child, and deaths.

The term "community" has more than one accepted meaning; here it refers not only to those beyond the immediate household who share with them kinship and religious ties, but also to the larger body of people living in a particular locality whose activities intersect on a

During the non-Hindu Lai Haraoba Festival, a group of Manipuri *maibis*, spirit mediums, dance and sing before the shrine of a local goddess, Lai Khurembi. In the course of the festival which can last for several weeks, the entire community participates in dances and dramas depicting ancient heroes such as Thoibi.

225

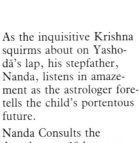

As the inquisitive Krishna squirms about on Yashodā's lap, his stepfather, Nanda, listens in amazement as the astrologer foretells the child's portentous future.

Nanda Consults the Astrologers. *18th century. Miniature painting, 12½ x 10″ (33 x 25 cm). National Museum, New Delhi.*

continuing basis and thus help to create a cohesive, interactive unit. Community performance events may thus involve a number of castes or groups who share many aspects of culture, including language, and have familiarity with music, dance, and other aspects of performance.

Public events are characterized by an heterogeneous audience of which the members may all have some appreciation of the event, but have little or no interrelationship with the performers or their fellow audience members.

All three performance levels continue to prevail in India, although success is increasingly being equated with the public sphere and its ultimate extension into the international performance setting.

Home Performance Events

Perhaps the most prominent of the home performances are those connected with the Hindu ritual stages of the life cycle referred to as *samskāra*s. Many of these stages are accompanied by songs sung by the women of the household. Beginning with childbirth—especially that of a male—women of many communities sing special songs to herald and bless the arrival of the new child. Not infrequently these songs describe the birth of Krishna, like this lullaby from Rajasthan, called *hālariyo:*

> The drum sounded in Mathurā,
> The birthplace of Krishna
> O my Lord, the news reached Gokul,
> Where Krishna spent his childhood,
> The son of the *dādhī* [a musician community] plays the drum.
> He brings auspicious news home, O my Lord. The *joshī*
>   [astronomer] also comes,
> Bringing the eternal message home.

Most Hindu communities have songs for the various stages in the marriage-pregnancy-birth part of the life cycle. The following cradle song, called *pālnā* in Maharashtra, describes each of the twelve days after birth leading to the child's naming ceremony.

On the first day, in the King's palace,
A child as vigorous as a lion is born.
It is the first incarnation of the lord Shiva as a child.
Ju bālā ju ju ne ju ju.

On the second day we go to the temple,
The child is decorated in many ways.
Beautiful maidens are cleaning it.
Ju bālā ju ju ne ju ju.

On the third day, bells are ringing,
There is joy throughout the town
And ladies all distribute sweets.
Ju bālā ju ju ne ju ju.

On the fourth day the child is decorated,
Important elders and uncles have come
And the child is fitting into society already.
Ju bālā ju ju ne ju ju.

On the fifth day ceremonies by the priests are done
The goddess comes and promises him success.
Ju bālā ju ju ne ju ju.

On the sixth day, earrings are put in his ears,
and a *tilak* of saffron and sandalwood on his forehead.
Ju bālā ju ju ne ju ju.

On the seventh day, religious observances are held
And white pearls are put on his cap.
Ju bālā ju ju ne ju ju.

On the eighth day, elders come to amuse the child
And five armed men stand guarding him.
Ju bālā ju ju ne ju ju.

On the ninth day, he wears a chain
With nine jewels and pearls.
The radiance of his beauty is everywhere.
Ju bālā ju ju ne ju ju.

On the tenth day, his picture is taken from upstairs
While the child sits on a blue horse.
Ju bālā ju ju ne ju ju.

On the eleventh day, he sits on an elephant
While five armed men stand guard.
Ju bālā ju ju ne ju ju.

On the twelfth day the namegiving ceremony is held
With great celebration,
And the child is named Shivajī.
Ju bālā ju ju ne ju ju.

These kinds of songs are sung by women, but some of them are also sung by male professional musicians, such those of the Langā and Manganhār communities in Rajasthan. Women also sing a variety of other songs, including festival songs and songs to accompany housework. These serve, in addition to their functional purpose, as outlets for self-expression. However, home events also include daily worship (*pūjā*) and devotional songs (*bhajan*) in which men play a prominent part. Men also take a leading role in the rites associated with the agricultural cycle and other work-oriented activities in which women might also participate.

So the child growing up in an Indian rural environment is naturally exposed to a variety of domestic performances, which, no doubt, he takes for granted. The occasional home events which involve specialist performers, like the snake charmers who might be called to catch a snake in the garden or the itinerant puppeteers, acrobats, or magicians who visit periodically, are the highlights of his experiential world. He may dread the visit of the shaman, Bhopā in Rajasthan or a Pulluvan in Kerala who performs a ceremony to cure ailing children by frightening away the evil spirits believed to possess the child. He may be indifferent to the intrusions of the family genealogist/bard and the mendicants who sing devotional songs in the hope of receiving alms. Yet, both will eventually shape his perceptions of the future.

From my childhood in the 1930s I recall visits from several astrologers who, unfolding sheafs of densely written and charted papers, generally predicted a great future for me. I also recall many animal acts—snakes and mongooses, bears and monkeys—and especially the visit of the acrobat who claimed he could walk on air and the marionette who smoked a cigar, coughing violently while emitting billows of smoke from his mouth, nostrils, and ears. Memorable events are obviously not the same for all Indian children, but virtually all have considerable exposure to the live performing world.

Community Performance Events

Community performances may be held in the central square of a village, a community hall, in temples or schools, in the home or garden of the village head or a wealthy person, or just in the street. Typically, an audience for such a performance consists of densely-packed crowds of every age, with the youngest boys seated at the front. Religious festivals, weddings, harvests, and important visitors are the primary occasions for these community events, which are often organized by a temple, a school, or the village *panchāyat* (council). Although the dramatic pageant *Rām-līlā*, which is presented annually in Ramnagar, and other similar events draw crowds from all over the country and can now hardly be considered as community events, many smaller performances take place in villages in connection with particular festivals. In the *Krishna-līlā* performances in Orissa, for example, traveling bands of performers of the Vālmīki community visit a number of villages on successive evenings to perform episodes from the Krishna story in the village squares.

Many community events involve mythological, historical, or romantic narratives in some form or another, the most common sources being the Rāmāyana, Mahābhārata and the Purānas, but there are also many others. The stories are presented in a variety of ways; the performers are seated on the ground and the story is conveyed primarily

Young boys and their fathers watch a group of snake charmers who are preparing to battle a mongoose (on top of the basket to the left) against a cobra.

Painting of a Snake Charmer. *19th century, miniature. Chandigarh Museum, Punjab.*

through narrative and song with instrumental accompaniment, minimal props and visual aids. The Langā musicians of Rajasthan sing many romantic ballads in this style, including the story of a boy (Dholā) and girl (Mārū) whose parents betroth them to each other even before they are born. When by chance they meet as youths and fall in love with each other, both know that they are married, but it is only after many ups and downs that they discover they are, in fact, married to each other.

There are many such romantic ballads in India, but there are also semi-historical epics in which the basic theme is that of courage and heroism, often ending in tragedy. The story of the brothers Ālhā and Udal, sung in Uttar Pradesh, relates basically historical events of the thirteenth century in north central India, just preceding the initial conquests of this area by the invading Muslims. Ālhā and Udal are generals in one of the three major kingdoms in north India at that time. The long epic describes the intrigues and battles among the three, which reach a climax when Ālhā abducts the daughter of his enemy, Prithvīrāj Chauhān of Delhi, who then sends an armed force to take revenge. Although Ālhā and Udal are slain in the resulting bloody battle, Prithvīrāj's forces emerge too depleted to resist the Muslim invasions that follow.

Left: Rādhā sits enchanted while Krishna plays the flute. On an open stage in Jaipur, these boys help to enliven the story of Krishna which their father is singing.

Above: Hereditary village bards from Rajasthan perform and sing at festivals and religious events sponsored by local landowners.

Manipuri revelers celebrate Holi with song and dance, drums and cymbals. Holi is a spring festival commemorating Krishna's destruction of the demoness Putanā and symbolically the end of winter. Kāma, the God of Pleasure, is the presiding deity and the playful throwing of color and jokes is infused with a bacchanalian air.

In some traditions, the main performer(s) stands and physical movement and dance are essential to the mode of expression. In Orissa, for instance, Dās Kāthiya is performed by two male performers who stand, playing wooden clappers, while they sing and narrate epic or Purānic stories. They periodically resort to dance movements, not only to enhance expression, but to experience and communicate the joys of rhythm and movement. While the main story line is taken from the traditional sources and has religious and moral content, the performers frequently interpolate humor, as well as social comment. This is illustrated by the following irreverent story narrated by the Dās Kāthiya bards in the middle of an episode from the Mahābhārata. The political nature of the story was motivated by the presence of a member of Parliament in the audience.

Once upon a time there was an old woodcutter, childless, blind and poor. His young wife, disgusted with his uselessness, threw him out of the house, whereupon he wandered helplessly about until he found a temple and there he found that people, thinking that he was a religious sādhu, gave him food and attended to his needs. Having nothing better to do, he began to meditate and pray. Gradually his powers of meditation increased, until he began to create tremors in the abode of the gods. Shiva, who was the prime minister of the heavenly parliament, did his best to ignore the tremors, but when finally their teacups started shaking, the other gods insisted that Shiva investigate the source of the problem. Reluctantly, Shiva descended to earth and sought out the old man, warning him that the intensity of his excessive piety was causing anxiety in the heavens. When this failed to have any effect, Shiva resorted to bribery, offering the old man the last remaining wish in the heavenly budget of the year, provided that the old man would tone down the intensity of his meditations. After some consideration the old man pronounced his wish, "I would like to see my son eating from a golden plate." Shiva was relieved that the problem had been solved so easily and readily granted the wish.

Upon returning to heaven, Shiva was greeted by his wife Pārvatī who immediately began chiding him on his gullibility. "What a fool you are! You idiot, can you not see! You have granted him not one wish, but three! First, he asks to see, and he is blind. Second, he asks for a son, and he has none. Third, he asks for a golden plate, and can you imagine a religious beggar having a gold plate?"

Then consternation reigned in heaven. Shiva had once again exceeded the budget! An emergency meeting of the gods was called. Shiva's reputation had to be protected and because the wish had already been granted, the inevitable occurred: a supplementary budget had to be approved (but not without opposition!).

These kinds of interpolations are not limited to just this tradition in Orissa, but are found in many others as well, and in order to elicit screams of delight, fear, or recognition from the children present, they are often made the object of these digressions.

In other community events of this nature, a visual prop may be employed. Often this takes the form of one or more paintings depicting the main events of the story being narrated. The *patuā* performers in Bengal make use of a series of small paintings, *pātā*, sequentially exposed during the performance. One of the best known examples is, however, found in Rajasthan, where a long scroll painting or *parh* about twenty feet long is hung behind the performers, whose narration, singing, music, and dance are collectively called *parh bānchnā* or parh reading.

One of the most prominent stories told in this way concerns the adventures of a minor Rajput chief of the fourteenth century, Pābūjī, who has since been deified by the local populace.

The boy Pābūjī was born to a magical woman who could transform herself into a lioness. Her husband deserted her upon discovering her powers, taking his son, but she vowed that one day she would become a black mare, and that her son Pābūjī would ride astride her into battle. When he reaches manhood, he borrows a black mare from the widow Deval Bai and after many thrilling adventures, he succeeds in capturing the reddish-brown camels promised as a dowry to his niece. He again borrows the mare for the horserace he must join during

Rajasthani Bhopā storytellers train their children at an early age to sing and dance the age-old story of Pābūjī, a Rajput chief.

his own marriage celebrations. He promises to come to Deval Bai's aid during the interim period should she require it. A message arrives just moments before the ceremony is completed, saying that Deval Bai's cattle are being rustled by his sister's husband Khīchī. He leaves the wedding before it is completed and rushes to the scene, where he recovers the cattle but spares Khīchī's life in order to save his sister from widowhood. Later Khīchī kills the merciful and dependable Pābūjī in a night ambush, as well as Pābūjī's brother, Buro, whose wife was pregnant. Before immolating herself on Buro's funeral pyre as was the custom at that time, she delivers the baby boy through a self-administered Caesarian. When the boy reaches the age of 12, he avenges his father's death, after which he renounces the world and retires to lead an ascetic life in the desert.

The performance requires at least two performers, commonly a male and a female. The male, called the Bhopā, accompanies himself on a type of fiddle called *rāvanahatta* and is the principal singer/story teller. The female (often his wife), called Bhopī, illuminates with an oil lamp the particular episode on the parh which is being described and also serves as supporting singer.

One can interpret the various forms of puppetry in India as extensions of the parh traditions, for animation brings the painted figures on the scroll closer to life. Marionette and shadow puppetry are most prominent in India, but the glove and rod forms are also found. The marionette form from Rajasthan, called *kathputlī*, usually presents the traditional story of the Rajput hero Amarsingh Rāthor and his conflict with the Mughal rulers in the mid-seventeenth century. The story is much abbreviated nowadays, with more emphasis being placed on the dancing girls, jugglers, snake charmers, and acrobatic horse riders—all, of course, puppets—who are depicted entertaining the royal court. Music for these shows includes one or more singers, drummers, and sometimes a melody instrument, the harmonium.

Shadow puppetry is found in many parts of India, including Orissa, Andhra Pradesh, Karnataka, and Kerala. Generally, it adopts the more conventional themes from the epics, particularly the Rāmāyana, with regional accretions to the stories and generous sprinklings of local humor.

Puppets come fully to life in the many types of dramas in India which employ masks or heavily painted faces and gargantuan headgear and costumes. Some of these, such as *kathakali* and *yakshagāna*, are well known in the West because of international tours by their troupes. Their accompanists, playing drums and wind instruments, are noted for their exceptional skill and large repertoire.

Some of the lesser-known performance traditions still continue in many parts of India as community events. Examples include the various forms of *teyyam* in Kerala, the *bhūta* dances in Karnataka, *chau* (recently "discovered" by urban and Western audiences), and *gambhīrā* in Bengal, each with its own unique musical ensemble. Although these forms are relatively unknown to the outside world, they are intimately tied to the lives of the people of these regions, including the children who are raised on them.

Several of these masked dances are connected with exorcism, trance, divination, curing, purification, and appeasement of evil spirits, sometimes with a child or young boy or girl as the trance medium. Other community performance traditions which involve these same purposes eschew facial masks, evidently accomplishing their ends by "masking" voices or producing bizarre sounds on fabulous instruments to represent the voices of spirits. Trance chanting, such as that of the Maibis in Manipur at the Lai Haraoba Festival (page 225), uses extraordinary techniques of voice production undoubtedly designed to communicate not with man, but with God. Similar goals account for the strange instrumental sounds produced by

A south Indian shadow puppet of Rāvana with ten heads and ten sets of arms.

Folk Art. Puppet of Rāvana. *Contemporary. Painted papier mâché, 28 x 19¼" (72 x 50 cm). Asutosh Museum of Indian Art, Calcutta.*

This elegant marionette depicts the heroine Queen Nāyakā who is an important character in many south Indian folktales.

String Puppet of Nāyakā. *Contemporary. Painted wood and cloth, 43 x 13½" (113 x 35 cm). Chitrakala Parishad, Bangalore.*

the Pulluvan community in their snake rituals (*sarpam pāttu*) in Kerala, where the songs are accompanied by a plucked drum, called *kudam*, which sounds something like a croaking frog; and many other "adventures in sound production" found in India. On the one hand, these illustrate the spirit of experimentation and innovation of India's performers in years gone by; on the other they reflect the importance of sound across the spectrum of traditional Indian society.

One must keep in mind that India has many community folk-dances, such as *bhangra* (page 221) in the Punjab and *garba* in Gujarat, performed at religious and seasonal festivals in which children may participate along with adults. Other community performance traditions which are designed to astound or amaze the viewer may have no particular religious or didactic bent. These include the animal acts, snake charmers, magicians, acrobats, jugglers, balancers, and other performers of novelty acts. A community event has a special impact on the child as it is usually more spectacular than the home events, usually lasts late into the night, and provides an opportunity to meet with school and other friends.

Public Performance Events

Certain community events have been extracted from their original environments and presented to more heterogeneous audiences live in large cities and on television. This applies particularly to most of the so-called classical traditions of music and dance in India. For instance, Indian classical music was once a chamber music limited primarily to temples and to the palaces and mansions of kings and noblemen, while the south Indian dance tradition, *bhārata nātyam*, was formerly a temple dance tradition. Both of these are now commonly seen on the concert stage and on television and are no longer limited to particular communities, regions, or even the country of origin, since they are increasingly being performed abroad. These classical traditions can be extremely important to the growing child, for it is in childhood that training must begin in order to master the arts.

It is interesting to note that proponents of particular non-classical performing traditions in India frequently seek to achieve "classical" status for them. This means not only that the tradition becomes recognized on a national and perhaps international level, but implies that it has achieved a type of artistic excellence which can be communicated beyond the community, and is thus suited to performance on the concert stage, national and even international television. The founding of schools for instructing children is a recognized step in the "classicization" of such forms.

Kuchipudi, the ancient dance tradition of Andhra Pradesh has now become a popular classical dance. Here, Rāja and Rādhā Reddy perform an episode from the story of Rādhā and Krishna.

Two further types of public performances need to be mentioned. Many regional performance traditions can be described as public events although they continue to remain as regional forms of expression and have not acquired a pan-Indian character, at least partly because of language barriers. Dramatic forms in regional languages (which invariably incorporate music and song), e.g., Marathi *nātak* and *tamāshā*, Rajasthani *khyāl*, Gujarati *bhavai*, are attended by heterogeneous audiences drawn from different localities within the linguistic area. Another category of public performance events are those not presented on a stage. The Rām-līlā at Ramnagar is an excellent example, as the performance action takes place at a number of different venues in the town and the procession from one to the other is very much a part of the performance. A procession is also the major feature of religious festivals such as the car festival of *Jagannāth* in Puri and the *Ganpati* Festival in Maharashtra. Also deserving of mention are the many melās (fairs) and *urs* (anniversary celebrations) held at shrines of saints. At Sufi shrines, for instance, a number of *qawwālī* and *darvesh* song events may be performed concurrently throughout the night. A particularly interesting feature of mysticism in India is that it serves as a meeting ground for Hindus and Muslims; indeed, melās and urs are often attended by both groups.

The reader should keep in mind that the purpose of the foregoing discussion has not been to provide a comprehensive list of performance traditions in India, which would be an impossible task, but to convey a sense of the importance of performance in India and to provide a glimpse of its variety in many regions.

For the Indian child the big melās and festivals are momentous occasions, very much like the Rose Bowl and other parades in the United States. Watching from the sidelines, the noise, excitement, and the participation of thousands of lay people, among whom may be their fathers, brothers, or relatives, surely heightens their expectation of admittance into the adult world.

The Performers

With such a wide variety of performance types in India, it is not surprising that there is also a great variety of performers whose life styles differ quite markedly. In India's villages, and to some extent in the larger urban centers, the family unit, often supported by members of the community, plays a fundamental role in performances involving the life cycle. Ritual events of the cycle are invariably consecrated by the songs and actions of the womenfolk, who are on occasion joined by priests and other specialist performers. By preserving age-old traditions, the Brāhman priests have also achieved for themselves an unique place in society. Their activities are, however, directed solely at the "upper" strata of society, the *dvija* or "twice-born," which, in addition to their own community, includes the Kshatriya and the Vaishya, who have traditionally been the most affluent of the Hindu groups in the country. The Shūdra were traditionally the equivalent of serfs; many of them have been expected to provide services, including the presentation of performances, for the upper classes. Although these performers have frequently won respect for their skills, they have generally continued to be regarded as low castes and are referred to by derogatory terms such as *mangat* (beggars). Nonetheless, individuals and communities involved in performance, particularly those involved in the performance of classical traditions and modern film music, have frequently succeeded in elevating their rank. For the most part, however, village performers have been grossly discriminated against.

Kathakali Dance School in Kerala, where young boys begin the rigorous training that is needed to perform this extremely formal and strict dance technique.

Above: After purifying rituals and worship to patron deities, a kathakali dancer aided by an apprentice begins the long and painstaking process of putting on his makeup and costume. A folded paper "beard" is glued to his chin and his face is painted to indicate the character he is to dance. Green symbolizes a hero or god.

Left: As drummers beat out a staccato rhythm, a kathakali dancer, wrapped in voluminous robes and adorned with elaborate jewelry and a massive crown, enacts the sacred mythology of the Hindu tradition.

The following discussion will be oriented toward one remarkable group of performers who live in Shadipur, a suburb of Delhi, with only occasional comments about other performers to provide perspective. The members of this community are principally from rural areas who have migrated to Delhi in search of new "patronage." Most of them are from Rajasthan which is adjacent to Delhi, but there are also some from other states as far away as Maharashtra and Andhra Pradesh, more than a thousand miles away. They have moved to Delhi and other cities because traditional forms of patronage could not continue to support them. In the cities they hope to find new patrons, especially among the tourists, and also opportunities to perform on radio, television, and in films.

It is important to understand that performance often requires a great deal of expertise which can only be developed through many years of practice, and thus it is usually relegated to those who are prepared to devote the time and effort needed to become specialists.

Performance specialists in rural India can be grouped in terms of life style: the resident performer, the itinerant performer, the nomadic performer, and the seasonal/occasional performer.

The resident performer is usually found in a kind of feudal system, called *jajmānī*, which is exemplified in Rajasthan. The performer, along with the barber, blacksmith, sweeper, etc., is here recognized as one of the "service providers" for the patron (*jajmān*), generally the village head, and other affluent members of the community. The derogatory term, mangat, is often applied in this context to such service providers. Performing groups of this kind in Rajasthan include Langā, Manganhār, Dholī, and Dādhī, who are musicians, and Bhāt and Chāran, who are genealogists and bards. The primary duty of the musicians is to perform at the patron's family life cycle events, childbirth, weddings, etc., in exchange for a portion of the patron's harvest. When required to perform on other occasions—for instance, when guests are to be entertained—they might receive additional remuneration in cash or animal stock. Weddings are particularly important occasions for them, providing opportunities to perform for, and to receive the largesse of, guests from outside the village.

The jajmānī musicians of Rajasthan are singers and instrumentalists. A significant part of their repertoire consists of ritual songs, many of which are probably derived from the songs sung by the women of the families in the privacy of their quarters. Their presentations are directed at the male members of the community, however, and they thus serve as communication links between the male and female worlds, which—among the traditionally dominant Rajput community at least—are in many ways greatly restricted. It is interesting

to note that many of these musicians are Muslims, although their patrons are often Hindus. In the past decade or two, females of the Muslim jajmānī performing communities of Rajasthan (especially Manganhārs) have been discouraged from performing in front of males for reasons of modesty as prescribed by Islam. One only finds female singers now among the Hindu Dholīs and Bhāts in Rajasthan, and even they generally cover their faces while singing in the presence of men.

The jajmānī system is strongest in the relatively isolated areas of western Rajasthan where desert and semi-desert conditions prevail. In addition to their principal occupation of making music, these resident musicians also rear horses and sometimes camels to supplement their incomes. Even in small villages of twenty or thirty houses in western Rajasthan, it is not unusual to find one or more houses belonging to these musicians. Some of them have a number of patrons in different villages which they visit periodically, usually on horseback. Their lives can sometimes be precarious, particularly in times of drought, which are not infrequent in Rajasthan.

Even so, the resident performers have enjoyed a measure of security over the years, since their regular patrons have, for the most part, recognized their responsibilities to them. But many performers either do not have this kind of regular patronage or are unable to sustain themselves exclusively on it. These performers are obliged to find patrons as best they can and hence become itinerant performers. The Bhāt community of Rajasthan, many of whose members reside now in Shadipur, has a particularly interesting and revealing background. It is principally a community of genealogists who periodically visit their

These young boys will inherit the *jajmāni* rights and responsibilities of their fathers; to sing and perform for patron landlords and to receive a portion of the harvest.

Jagdish Bhāt and Mohan Bhāt, kathputlī puppeteers from Rajasthan, demonstrate the technique of manipulating marionette puppets.

regular patrons to record births, marriages, and deaths. There are two kinds; *bahibānchā*, who maintain written records, and *mukh pāth*, who maintain records orally and who also often compose or recite poetry and tales. Both these groups would be considered as resident performers because they have fixed abodes and regular patrons, even though they are frequently on the move. Certain Bhāts have taken up a different line of performance, that of kathputlī marionette puppetry, and it is this group which is most prominent in Shadipur. Evidently, these performers needed supplementary income and thus created or adopted the marionette tradition, becoming itinerant performers.

Itinerant performers generally also have permanent abodes and often a small piece of farming land to which they return, particularly during the monsoon season. Nomadic performers, on the other hand, have no permanent home to return to. They are sometimes referred to as *khānābadosh* (which translates literally as "having his house on his back"), particularly in Pakistan. Information on these itinerant and nomadic performers is relatively scarce and often conflicting. They are called by many specific names and often in different regions by the same name, or obvious derivatives, e.g., *Dom*, (which has been equated with *Rom*, or gypsy) *Dum*, *Dumbāru*, *Dumbu*, etc. Some even have similar performance traditions, but it is not clear whether a single original community of performers has dispersed through the country over the years or, alternatively, whether the generic name (whatever it might originally have been, Dom or Dumbu) represents an occupational group. This name and its variants, are found from the Punjab in the north, to Orissa and Bengal in the east, Rajasthan, Gujarat, and Maharashtra in the west and down into Andhra Pradesh in the south. Similarly, the name Nat and its derivates are also very widespread, but Nat or Nata, as we mentioned earlier, meant actor, dancer, or mime and is probably an occupational name. Nowadays, Nats are known largely as acrobats, balancers, tightrope walkers, and "strongmen." More than one Nat community is now found living in Shadipur and, although most of them are from Rajasthan, at least one family comes from Maharashtra.

The itinerant and nomadic groups seem to share a sense of community, probably because of the similarity of their life styles. The Bhāt puppeteers refer to twelve communities of peripatetic performers and artisans, called *bārā pāl* ("twelve tents"), or *sarkī band* ("straw-shelter dwellers"), with whom they have some affinity. The characteristic feature of these itinerant peoples, according to the Bhāt puppeteer Babu Lal, is that "they live in tents, use three stones for their cooking fire and a *tavā* (a type of frying pan) for cooking their food." But the depth of the shared affinity is not very clear. Evidently, the individual groups are basically endogenous, some Hindu, others Muslim. Even the number of groups given, twelve, may be symbolic rather than empirical, since R.V. Russell's *The Tribes and Castes of the Central Provinces of India* mentions that the Meo, the Muslim branch of the Mīnā tribe in Rajasthan, also recognize *bārā pāl*, in this case twelve clans, quite different from those of the itinerant peoples. In addition to the Bhāt and Nat communities in Shadipur, there are the animal trainers, Madārī or Qalandar, who train monkeys and bears, and Saperā or Jogī, who charm snakes; there are also Maslet magicians, Bahrūpiyā impersonators, Bhopā and Bhopī scroll storytellers, and a number of other groups who make toys, puppets, and the like.

The whole community in Shadipur is, in fact, geared to the world of the child and to the child in every adult. Among the most humorous of these performers are the Bahrūpiyā, who specialize in impersonations. (The word Bahrūpiyā means "one who takes many forms.") On one occasion, dressed (or rather undressed) as a savage with war paint and carrying a bow and arrow or spear, a performer holds a child audience fascinated as they follow him through the streets of a small town or village. Periodically he threatens them with his weapons, eliciting amusement as well as trepidation as they jump out of his line of sight, just in case. Alternatively, he may appear as a policeman, his threat to take one or more youngsters into custody greeted with great hilarity by the audience, but with some anxiety by the children he accosts.

While often directed at children, these performances often have undertones satirizing other communities and individuals, religious mendicants, businessmen, itinerant ironsmiths, and others. Some Bahrūpiyās claim once to have been resident performers, i.e., to have had regular patrons in the jajmānī system, who were obliged to become itinerant performers as their regular patronage weakened. They often say that they have fifty-two acts, called *sāng*, a word which is evidently related to *swāng* or *sāng*, dramatic forms found in Uttar Pradesh and Hariyana. The Bahrūpiyā's acts are, however, performed in the streets and not on a stage. The acts are meticulously conceived and presented in elaborate makeup and with ingenious (but portable) props. The purpose is often to deceive the people into believing that they are being confronted by the real thing—a doctor, policeman, tribesman, ironsmith, religious mendicant, salesman, or whatever.

It might appear that the act of the Pābūjī scroll storysingers, who also live in Shadipur, is not particularly directed at children and it is true that during the telling of their story they do not generally resort to humor or direct jokes to the children in the audience. Most of these singers belong to the Thorī community and are not only itinerant performers but also shamanistic healers, who are frequently

Using ingenious costumes a Bahrūpiyā impersonator plays the role of a young man carrying his aged father.

employed in their traditional environment to cure children's ailments. Their performance is considered to be a ritual one and is often commissioned when a child is ill in order to propitiate Pābūjī. There are many performance genres in India which serve similar functions for healing and fertility, some of which are performed annually in villages and others commissioned for specific purposes frequently connected with the child cycle.

Many other itinerant groups could also be mentioned, for example, the Kanjar who, among other activities make and peddle clay toys. Some of them are also musicians and dancers. A section of this community owns small, easily assembled wood and metal merry-go-rounds and makes its living through selling rides to children.

The seasonal or occasional performers of India are carpenters, tailors, farmers, etc., who are hired to perform for such occasions as festivals and weddings. In a sense, they are talented amateurs (although paid for these performances), since performance is not usually the principal livelihood of their families or communities. The distinction between these "amateurs" and members of hereditary performing communities who adopt new part-time vocations in response to diminishing rewards from performance is not always clear. Although Shadipur is occupied primarily by the hereditary performing communities, a significant number of talented "amateur" performers are dispersed throughout India.

The range of performing traditions in India and life styles followed by folk performers is vast. Many of these performances affect children, variously entertaining them, curing them in times of illness, or protecting them from dangerous spirits. They also expose the child from infancy to the world of the adult, including ritual and esoteric practices which might otherwise be unacceptable to them in later life. Performances also serve to celebrate and announce to the community the various stages of the child's life and to enhance anticipation of the "promise of the future" within the child.

The Changing Scene: Tradition and Innovation

Much has already been written about the impact of modernization and the mass media on the state of traditional performances in India and elsewhere. Most of this commentary has been negative and emotional, motivated by the desperate urgency of preserving the world's diverse cultural heritage before it vanishes irrevocably. While many performing traditions are rapidly decaying in India, others are flourishing as never before. We are witnessing a period of challenge for performers as well as for governments, institutions, and concerned individuals. If we care enough for our heritage to carry out archaeological digs and preserve ancient monuments, should we not also dedicate our efforts to preserving human repositories of the ancient arts and crafts—not so much the objects themselves, but the knowledge of the old ways of doing? To save animal species from extinction, we provide large areas for national parks and animal preserves; why not also preserves for the dying cultural traditions of humanity? Some scholars believe that we should not interfere with the normal flow of progress, but can the pervasive influence of mass media be considered part of the normal flow of progress? Change is inevitable, and it is scholarly conceit to believe that we can make more than a minor impact on the process of change, particularly against the powerful and widespread influence of mass media. It is thus imperative that we now make a concerted effort, enlisting government and institutional aid wherever possible.

Meanwhile, it should not be thought that performers have been sitting by idly waiting for the inevitable. Many groups have been aggressive in seeking new patrons and adapting their performances to the changing environment through innovation and experimentation. Marionette puppeteers are devising new techniques of puppet construction and manipulation, increasing the number of strings for greater articulation, and introducing new acts with new characters, as well as trying new media, such as glove puppetry. The Langā and Manganhār musicians are learning new instruments and new genres of songs to reach a wider audience. One might be tempted to think that these performers are abandoning their hoary traditions, but no one likes to give up one's own inheritance and they are no exception. The recent innovations often show great ingenuity on the part of the performers when they embed old materials in the guise of the new.

To conclude this article, I would like to give a concrete example to illustrate the resourcefulness of the Indian performer. Kathputlī puppeteers who have migrated to Shadipur and to other large cities have had to find new patrons. Among those they have found are advertisers of products and banks who want to encourage the Indian population, particularly those in villages, to save and to borrow money for tractors and other equipment. Puppeteers are being hired to travel from village to village entertaining the villagers while presenting their new patrons' message. To this end they have introduced new characters and new acts. One such show begins, after some entertaining preliminaries, with the arrival in the village of a modern puppet character, a bank representative named Munīm (accountant), who explains the advantages of a bank loan to the village head. A decadent ex-nawāb, smoking a cigarette (and puffing frantically) patiently listens to the arguments and finally interrupts, shaking his head, "What has this world come to? It was not like this in my time. I would just snap my fingers and Chāndbībī (a courtesan) would appear to dance for me." At this moment, a traditional female dancer arrives on the stage to dance for him. After she completes her dance and leaves the stage, the nawāb continues his reminiscences as, one by one, the old acts are performed just as he remembers them. At the conclusion of the reveries, the case for the bank investments is continued, virtually as though there had been no discontinuity between the old and the new.

The ancient image of Krishna playing the flute is still repeated today as a young cowherd plays a lilting tune on his bamboo flute.

Fig. 1. Related to the abstract ritual floor drawings of Bihar is the abstract and, at the same time, phallic design of the kohbar, the central motif drawn on the wall of the ceremonial marriage chamber by the women painters of Mithilā. The same design is drawn on the marriage proposal given by the young woman to the man of her choice. *Contemporary, Mithilā, Bihar.*

The Ritual Arts of India
Stella Kramrisch

The Ritual Arts of Women: Tracings on the Floor

The home into which a child is born and where he or she grows up
and becomes an adult stays with the person through life wherever it
may be spent. In a traditional Indian household domestic rites accompany every stage of life from even before birth. They celebrate, con-
firm, and smooth the stages of the path of the growing mind. The
sacraments of life, the seasonal festivals of the gods in the rhythmic
order of the cosmos, and the biological sequence within the human
condition are ever-recurring moments, each marked by the proper
rites.

Domestic ritual art is an essential aspect of these celebrations.
Throughout Hindu India it is practiced only by women in the form of
drawings on the floor (Fig. 2). Walked on by family and friends, the
drawings become blurred and are extinguished to be renewed—some
of them, like the kolam designs of south India, every morning, while
others on each of the celebrations that are part of the sacraments or
rites of passage accompanying the child's existence from the womb
through adulthood: birth, the boy's investiture with the sacred thread,
and marriage. Others are drawn as acts of devotion when taking a vow
(*vrata*) to achieve a desired result. Although the rites of passage (*samskāra*) are performed pre-eminently for the male child in the largely
patriarchal Hindu society, all members of a household are visually and
magically affected by the ongoing practice of ritual art: it molds their
minds, assuages their souls, and gives strength to their hearts.

These purely abstract drawings are known under different names in
the different parts of the country: *māndnā* in Rajasthan, *rangolī* in
Gujarat and Maharashtra, *sathya* in Saurashtra, *aripan* or *aypan* in
Bihar, *aipan* in the Kumaon, *ālpanā* in Bengal, *jhunti* in Orissa, *caukā
rangāna* or *cauk pūrna* or *sonarakhna* in Uttar Pradesh, *muggū* in
Andhra Pradesh, *kolam* in south India.

Classified in Sanskrit texts but hardly accounted for in the history
of Indian art, floor drawing is diametrically different from Indian art
in its well-known aspects.[1] It has none of the sensuous plasticity of
biomorphic form in which classical Indian sculpture and painting have
captured the breath of living beings and the sap of vegetation, none of
the jewel-smooth planes in which Indian painting of the last centuries
presented melodies and romance. These forms of art, sacred and monumental the one, courtly yet intimate the other, are not linked with

the ephemeral patterns of the floor tracings drawn by Hindu women. The art of drawing on the floor is a discipline that carries inventiveness from generation to generation. Its traditions, handed down from mother to daughter, constitute a mark of achievement for each succeeding generation. A young girl's training begins in her fifth or sixth year, and she reaches competence in her twelfth year.

The art of drawing on the floor is practiced by women of the Brāhman and Kāyashtha castes. Women learned it ultimately from traditions more ancient than those of the Aryan Brāhmans and they elaborated them in forms by which the floor is covered with the magic potency in patterns peculiar to each part of India. The material used in these diagrams, rice powder, is felt to have magical powers. It scares away evil spirits.[2] Within the confines of the more or less intricate geometry of the diagram, an invoked presence finds its allotted place. Its power is confined and thereby held in its place and for the purpose for which the diagram was drawn.

The visual effect of these symbolic shapes is at one with their efficacy. They not only form abstract patterns, they are the concentrated forms of mind and will. They are diagrams intuited and transmitted by women.

If to this day throughout practically the whole of India different abstract designs belong to different regions of this ephemeral art, ancient monuments and artifacts bear sporadic witness to the range of this non-objective, non-representational art. It is without image, figure, or narrative.

Carved in stone as part of architectural monuments, such as the railing of the Stupa of Bharhut of the second century B.C. or large areas of the casement panels of the Dhamekh Stupa at Sarnath of the seventh century A.D., indefinitely extensible patterns centered on the motif of the swastika are representative of a world of Indian art that co-exists but does not intermingle with the "physioplastic" representational or narrative art forms full of figures having human, animal, or plant shape[3,4]. The indefinitely extensible designs based on the swastika of the Buddhist monuments at Bharhut and Sarnath are not the only Indian abstract designs of great antiquity. Hexagons, hexagrams, and the four-"petaled" square form contiguous ground covers such as the one painted on an earthen jar from Harappa of the mid-second millennium B.C. Elsewhere, in a circular panel from Basarh of the fourth century A.D., a hexagonal concatenation of spirals is centered on a six-"petaled" motif.[5,6]

Indefinitely extensible patterns are not confined to India. In China, the principle of the indefinitely extensible pattern is seen applied to the body of a ritual bronze vessel assignable to the late eleventh or

Fig. 2. The rice paste that flows from the finger of the artist onto the ground translates her inner vision and experience into visible form. Here an urban housewife, somewhat removed from her traditional role, is creating a pattern for a decoration.

Fig. 3. In a māndnā drawing, every part of the circular or polygonal area is linked with the center.

Pherbāja or Vārpher-Kā-Kherā. Māndnā. Holi Festival. Bundi District, Rajasthan.

early tenth century B.C.[7] It is a pattern of interlocked "T" hooks. Another kind of indefinitely extensible motif is a squared, meander-like spiral adjusted to filling and enriching the curved planes of other pre-Anyang and Anyang bronzes.[8] Although not going back to a past as remote as that of the Chinese bronzes, abstract art as floor decoration is represented also in the West, in classical antiquity, as seen in a mosaic from the pavement of the Domus Augustana, built under Domitian on the Palatine in Rome between A.D. 81 and 96, centuries before Islam covered the walls of its sanctuaries with the intricacies of abstract, geometric design executed in wood, stone, and tiles.[9]

The geometrical designs lent themselves to being copied or adjusted to different techniques. Various techniques, on the other hand, particularly plaiting and weaving, might have stimulated the visual imagination of the designer of the floor tracings. They did not, however, detract her hand and eye from the steady flow of the even line of her work on the floor (Fig. 2). Their contact is direct. No brush, no tool of any kind intervenes between the hand of the artist and the ground onto which the rice paste flows from her finger. A small cloth soaked in this liquid medium is held in her right hand and when squeezed allows the pigment to flow from her finger in a steady, thin flux. This direct contact of finger, paint, and ground allows the direct translation from her inner vision and experience into visible form.

Different from the widespread Indian practice by women of nonfigurative ritual drawings on the floor are the ritual, figurative wall paintings executed by the women of the region of Madhuban in Bihar, on the occasion of a wedding. Colorful and rich in symbols, they are replete with mythical content. These wall paintings glorify the *kohbar*, a room decorated and made auspicious for the nuptial rites. In its spontaneity and immediacy this local style of painting abounds in a variety of form created by the practicing individual artists. The wealth and splendor of these "Madhubani" paintings highlights the Aditi exhibition. Their tradition—in its almost miraculous rebirth—is figurative, though its central symbol, the *linga*, is here an effloresence of an abstract design, whether it is depicted in the midst of figures on the walls of the kohbar, or on a sheet of paper as the central motif of the marriage proposal (Fig. 1). The imageless tracings on the floor on the other hand, make visible a creative activity different in kind from that of representation and narrative.

The Māndnā of Rajasthan

The richest and most complex variety of abstract designs belongs to Rajasthan, where the name of this domestic ritual art is māndnā.[10]

Fig. 4. Traversing intersecting strips pass above and then below each other in this māndnā.

Khera. Māndnā. Bundi District, Rajasthan.

Fig. 5. Paglyā designs float freely around the larger māndnā. This paglyā, like a māndnā, is surrounded by freely floating symbols. *Solah Bījanī-Kā-Paglyā. Māndnā. Bundi District, Rajasthan. Dīpāwalī Festival.*

Fig. 6. This paglyā design appears to be composed of links in a chain as its name *sānkal* indicates. The design suggests the spire of a shrine and evokes the chariot of the sun, newly born from the dark half of the year, on its northern course. The form of the structure is linked with interlacing Moebius strips. This kind of paglyā is drawn in a corner of a room, as a rule, and is not meant to be trodden on. Visually, the design is three dimensional.
Sānkal-Kā-Paglyā. Māndnā. Village Talera, Bundi District, Rajasthan.

The most significant of the motifs of māndnā drawings is a circular or polygonal area of which every part is linked with the center. The discrete fields into which the area of the māndnā is divided are bordered not by a single but by a double line, which has the effect of a strip or band that separates as much as it connects adjacent fields. These are occupied by indefinitely extensible patterns. They play a secondary role in the overall design of the māndnā. Its principles are radiation from the center and interweaving of the radiating areas by means of the circumambient strips (Fig. 3). This linear or rather planar design often has a layered effect of tiers compacted and traversed by the intersecting strips (Fig. 4). At the corners of the māndnā they—like the Moebius strip—appear to turn upon themselves, the inside becoming the outside of the strip (Fig. 3). Within the māndnā the strips intersect and appear interwoven, the same strip passing now above and then below the other.

Māndnās are drawn on the ground of house and courtyard, in village and town. The ground, prior to the drawing of the māndnā, generally has been painted red.[11] The white māndnās are laid out like lace, enhancing the festive mood of the occasion.

The different types of māndnā design are known by names such as "town," "market place," or "well." The affinity of the geometrical diagrams of ground and site plans with māndnā designs extends also to the *yantra*. The latter are axial diagrams serving as ritual tools and aids in meditation and concentration.

A māndnā is as a rule surrounded by other smaller motifs, among which the "footprint" or *paglyā* (Figs. 5, 6, and 7) is a bilateral figure. While the māndnā is centered, the paglyās and the other free-floating devices around the māndnā contribute an outer zone around the māndnā (Fig. 7) and sometimes also around a paglyā (Fig. 5).[12,13] Sometimes cusp-like devices (*laddu*) adhere to the periphery of a māndnā (Fig. 7).[14] As a rule, each "protective" border device is filled with a field of one or the other indefinitely extensible pattern. Such trellis-like patterns—akin to and having absorbed Islamic indefinitely extensible patterns—also fill the several areas of the māndnā. It is as saturated in its seemingly multilevel richness as it is controlled by the rigorous plan of the entire design. Different māndnās are drawn for different celebrations and every locality has its own version of each type of māndnā.

The center of the main māndnā has its position in the center of the courtyard of the house. Paglyā motifs or footprints (Figs. 5 and 6), although they may not be recognizable as such, are placed outside the closed order of the central "town," or "market place," where they introduce an element of direction and possibly an indication of the arrival and auspicious presence of Lakshmī, the goddess of fortune, wealth, and well-being. In the floor drawings outside Rajasthan, and particularly in the floor tracings of ālpanā designs in Bengal, the curvacious and clearly recognizable footprints of the goddess are arrayed along her path (Fig. 8). In the paglyās of Rajasthan, however, nothing but the name suggests the association with the feet; although merely verbal, it is the only anthropomorphic reference in the repertory of māndnā design. (See also Fig. 6.)

The names of the different types of māndnā are labels by which a māndnā is recognized. They do not explain its form. A māndnā has no other purpose than to make its auspicious appearance at the time of the appropriate celebration. Its interlocked strips or pathways define the total design laid out on the floor. It flows from the finger of the artist right on to the ground. While as a rule it depicts no object, it traces the pathways and movements of the artist's mind. Within the discipline of a tradition, the creative mind of the artist traces its own movement on several levels, all rich in content and interlinked in such a way that what is above at one point is also below at another, and what is inside here is immediately also outside there. It is the making of this pattern, its creation, that matters. Creativity here is in tune with the rhythms of sun and moon, the seasons in the cosmos, and the sacraments in the life of man.

Mehndī   Its instrument is the mind and hand of woman. The hand itself, in turn, becomes the ground for symbolic drawings like those on the floor. Here the design flows henna red from the tip of the woman artist's finger onto the palm of the woman to be decorated. Here, in the art of mehndī, which means henna, the repertory of symbolic geometric māndnā designs is applied and augmented, eroticized, and trivialized by the addition of folk art figures of plant, bird, fish, and other auspicious objects down to the fingertips stained solidly with the red "love juice" of mehndī, generating and proclaiming married love.   Neither unmarried girls nor pregnant women should be decorated in this manner. The modification of the māndnā tradition, carrying a load of meaning on diverse levels in its use as erotically stimulating decoration, converts ritual artistic tradition into conventionally applied symbolism.

Born in a household where people take delight in but also walk on māndnās, paglyās, and other related designs that have accrued in the artist's mind around symbols such as the cross, the swastika, the hexagram, and the lotus flower, a child held and caressed by his mother's hand decorated with mehndī absorbs the unspoken message of these

Fig. 7. The circle of this māndnā is mounted with 16 round cusp-like figures called *laddu*.

Gatthā-kā-ātha Phul.
Māndnā. Dīpāwalī Festival.
Bundi. Rajasthan.

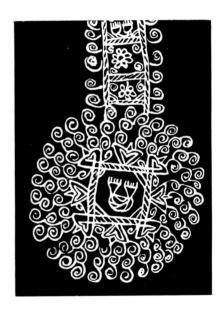

Fig. 8. In this floor drawing from the Punjab Hills, the footprints of the goddess Lakshmī are clearly recognizable.

251

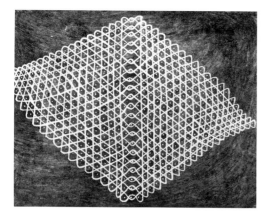

Figs. 9 and 10. The dot in the center of the loops formed by the unbroken lines symbolizes the seed—the source of life.

designs and their rhythms. If the child is a daughter she will learn to create a ground of beauty which, in turn, she herself will be able to prepare and pass on.

The Rite of Hīr Māndnās are drawn on auspicious occasions of the cosmic cycle of the year and the life cycle—they must not be drawn when a death has occurred in the house—but they are most lavish in the celebration of marriage and at Dīwālī, the festival of lights. If the women's ritual art of māndnā enriches and sanctifies life by abstract form, the rite of hīr, "the passing of the torch of knowledge," enacted by men only, is explicit in its meaning. This ritual is performed on the evening of Dīwālī, after the drawing of the māndnās, and the worship of the goddess Lakshmī. The hīr, a lighted pot filled with oil and serving as a kind of torch, is carried—in the Harauli region of southern Rajasthan—by the younger male members of the family to their elders, who will replenish the oil so that the torch keeps burning. The young generation will carry forward this "torch of illumination" with the blessing of the elders to dispel the dark night of their souls. It is essential to kindle the light of illumination for every male member in the family. The hīr ritual for a newly born male child has a special significance, for it will illuminate the path of his life. When Lakshmī pūjā is over, the newborn is carried, along with his hīr, to his elders. The hīr is included among the small lesser motifs surrounding a māndnā or paglyā. Participation of the newborn child in the performance of the hīr ritual will leave its impress on the infant's mind; as part of the ambience of the māndnā or paglyā on the floor, the hīr is drawn as a circle to which is attached a rectangular pointed shape in the style of a māndnā design (Fig. 7).

Kolam and Muggū of South India

In south India the tracings on the floor are called kolam in Tamil Nadu, and their place is at the threshold of the house, a zone of passage from the known—the house—to the unknown outside. This zone is protected by the design traced on the floor in an unbroken line forming loops and enclosures each marked by a dot in its center (Figs. 9 and 10), the dot being a symbol of the seed, the source of life. In southern India, the dot as a symbol of the seed and origin of life is also a symbol of the Mother Goddess. Archana Shastri, in his *Language of Symbols*, reports that the dominant motif in the villages of Andhra is the dot arranged meticulously all around the inner walls of the houses.[15] In Telengana, Andhra, Karnataka, and Tamil Nadu, the thresholds are mainly dotted in red and yellow. The vermillion dot "is a potent symbol—the archetypal meaning of which is associated with blood—the source of life and the primordial Mother Goddess." In Andhra Pradesh the floor tracings are called muggū. Here, and in Karnataka, the line takes the shape of the serpent, the waves of its body ensconce the dot (Fig. 11). In Karnataka, the convolutions of the body of the serpent are laid out around the serpent's head. The dots here are given the shape of pentagrams (Fig. 12).

Dot and snake are the most potent symbols of fertility and regeneration. The theme of the serpent gives mythical definition to the wavy lines of the drawing on the floor. They glide with geometrical assurance in and out of the loops of configurations which consist of one uninterrupted, continuous linear movement. It conveys the serpent power of the Goddess, and the dots corroborate her presence.

Fig. 11. In Andhra Pradesh, the unbroken line is in the shape of a serpent, the waves of its body ensconcing the dot.

The Ālpanā of Bengal

The presence of deity conveyed by myth and legend has its support in the drawings on the floor. The interaction of the visual and the verbal tradition is strong in the art of the ālpanā, the floor drawings of Bengal. This is especially true when, as is frequently the case, they anticipate the fulfillment of the wish and the vow (vrata) of the young girl who draws them. Vratas are solemn vows; they demand observances such as fasts, chastity, and the performance of acts—expected to fulfill the wish for the sake of which they are performed. They are projections of desires into form and action; the very act of giving form to them leads to their fulfillment. Ālpanās are spellbinding devices; by their indwelling energy they trap the desired object. Their magic has an ancient past. It ensures the fertility of the fields, of the cattle and in the house. Emblematic shapes of great ingenuity like that of the goddess Shashtī, presiding deity of childbirth and protectress of children are visual spells (Fig. 13).[16] They lead to a happy life, a happy death. One such vow, the toshila vrata, ends its prayer with the wish "grant me to die close to the sea."[17] In another vrata, the sejuti vrata, the goddess of evening is worshipped. The vrata necessitates forty different ālpanās before each of which a flower and song are offered. One of the songs addresses a sparrow: "Sparrow, oh sparrow, the river is about to overflow—I shall build my house on a height whence I shall see the rice fields grow ripe. They will bring me bags full of gold."[18]

The sea and river are vital powers. Their billowing waves harbor danger; they bring fertility. They have to be prayed to and assuaged. The estuary of the Ganges, the most sacred of all the rivers in India, is in Bengal. The river is worshipped as the goddess Gangā, who gives

Fig. 12. In Karnataka, the unbroken line takes the form of a convoluted serpent around which are dots in the shape of a pentagram.

Fig. 13. The goddess Shashtī, who protects children, is represented in this ālpanā.

life's joys and brings Release. The waves fecundate the land, ripples of water run through the young green fields. Waves are the most vital theme of the ālpanā design. That is why the ups and downs of the wavy lines are filled with various kinds of vegetation, most notably the lotus. The wave of the lotus rhyzome is an ancient theme of Indian art, most tellingly elaborated in the relief frieze of the railing of Bharhut in the second century B.C., and in Ajanta of the fifth century A.D., where the most ravishing lotus flowers were painted with dew-fresh perfection. The recurrent theme of the wave as a formative principle of composition runs through the whole of Indian art. Its versions in ālpanā designs are inventive and varied, not only concerned with the flower—its open bloom generally is central to the layout of kānthā textiles—but also with the fruits of the fields, the richness of the harvest (Fig. 14). Ālpanā design excels in flowing curves and is less abstract than māndnā design.

Kānthā Textiles

Closely related in their design to that of the ālpanā floor drawings are the kānthās. Their ingeniously devised embroidery technique raises to the level of art the frequently artless configurations seen in ālpanā drawings. The kānthā, a patched cloth—kānthā means rag—was made mainly in eastern Bengal (Bangladesh) but also in Bihar, of worn-out and disused saris and dhotīs. After becoming threadbare, their thin, white cotton cloth with its colored borders was cut, patched, quilted, and embroidered. According to the thickness of the quilt and its size, it was used as a cover to be spread, as a wrap to be worn, or folded as a bag. The white ground of the quilt was embroidered and reinforced with colored threads drawn from the colored borders. The colors of the kānthās of the early part of the nineteenth century are mainly red and blue (Fig. 14); in the latter half of the century, yellows and greens are also included. The material of the kānthās are rags and their threads. Joined afresh, these tatters are given a new wholeness, and their embroidered designs spring from this meaning. The kānthā is a work that gives wholeness to things that were of no use any more, to fragments without any significance. This rite of the restitution of wholeness is a domestic one, performed by women, though rarely by Brāhman women. The more ornate kānthās are the work of the Kāyashtha, or middle-class women from the homes of clerks and scribes. However, women of all castes and classes of the rural population, including Muslim women, owned or had embroidered kānthās. They were given as presents within the family or to friends.

Fig. 14. The lotus flower, symbol of universal manifestation, occupies the center of this kānthā design.

Kānthā. *Early 19th century. Cotton embroidery on white quilt, 33 x 31" (83 x 81 cm). Khulna, East Pakistan.*

Textile symbolism in India is hallowed by tradition. In the Rig Veda and the Upanishads, the universe is envisioned as a fabric woven by the gods. The cosmos, the ordered universe, is one continuous fabric with its warp and woof making a grid pattern. Hence the importance of wholeness, not only of the uncut garment, like the sari or the dhotī, but also of the cloth woven all in one piece, on which a sacred picture is to be painted. Whether as cover for the body or as ground for a painting, the uncut fabric is a symbol of totality and integrity. It symbolizes the whole of manifestation. Inversely, rags are offered to the gods. Chindīya Deo, the lord of tatters, gives a new whole cloth if a rag is offered to him. There are rag shrines all over the country. Their goddess is Chithāriya Bhāvanī, Our Lady of Tatters. The rags are given a new wholeness. They clothe holiness.

The symbolism inherent in the patchwork of the kānthā is the ground, which is embroidered with nearly equal perfection on both sides. The act of making whole demands perfection throughout. The design is drawn by the embroiderer herself or by another woman. It is neither produced by a professional artist nor copied from anywhere. No two kānthās are ever alike; each is an original creation, although kānthās from a single district follow certain types and have more in common with each other than with those from more distant villages.

The design of the square or rectangular field of the kānthā, in principle, relies on a central circle occupied by a lotus flower, an ancient Indian symbol of universal manifestation and of this world in particular. Four trees mark the four corners of the central square around the lotus circle. The four trees are symbols of the four directions. The disc of the many-petaled lotus, when drawn as an ālpanā, on the floor, would support a vessel filled with water in the center. Deity is invoked and known to be present in a vessel filled with water. In the design of the kānthā, the entire ground of the quilted cloth between the lotus and directional trees is filled with figures, objects, symbolic devices, and scenes whose shapes and combinations are dictated by the imagination of the artist. In the marginal field around the central square, themes from ancient myths and legends are laid out next to scenes and figures commenting on contemporary life, and both are permeated with purely symbolic devices. The design of the kānthās provides wide margins for showing the contents of a woman's mind. Their figures and symbols are freely associated and rhythmically assembled.

Thematically, the art of the kānthā is an enriched textile version of the art of the aripan or ālpanā, the painting on the floor, its magic purpose being enhanced by the textile symbolism of its material and the way it is used. Stylistically, its form and effects are entirely its own, unique in the world of textile art.

While the art of the kānthā is essentially a rural art imbued with Hindu myths, it is also perceptive of the life of Bengal in the nineteenth century, with some of its manners and fashions derived from those of the West—an imaginative blend of the actuality of living where every day contributes some novelty to be absorbed by the stream of the tradition and integrated into its style. It is an art of leisure. Sophisticatedly primitive, the quilt of the kānthā integrates many layers of the fabric of Indian life, tribal as well as urban, in its thoughtful conception.

The magic that underlies its purpose is that of love, not coercion—unlike that of the diagrammatic floor drawings whose purpose is wish fulfillment. A kānthā is given as a present; it is conceived with an outgoing mind and brings the entire personality of the maker to the person for whom it is made. Its composition is a ritual, its symbols being laid out around the center of the lotus of manifestation in the four cosmic directions. To its whorls and waves, to the lotus and the life trees, are assigned the innumerable figured scenes of the mythic, everpresent past together with episodes of the passing scene. All of them are firmly stitched into a reconstituted, vibrant wholeness. The kānthā is the form, by textile means, of a creative process of integration within each woman who makes one.

The ritual arts practiced in the home by members of the family have contributed two essential components to the sum total of Indian art. These are the abstract magical designs, their patterns akin to *yantra*, the magical diagrams of Tantric ritual, drawn on the floor by women throughout India, and the other the tribal pictograms subsequently discussed. Both these forms of Indian art are created by nonprofessionals.

The Role of the Professional Craftsman

Professional artists did, however, supply the immense variety of objects that enrich the celebration of the samskāras and also made viable the access to the powers on which life was felt to depend. The professional practitioners were mostly hereditary craftsmen trained in their traditions from an early age. They were organized in guilds and practiced their calling according to the exigencies of local conditions while applying the standards of their training. These were laid down in scriptures, and their rules controlled the adequacy of production. To this day, in those areas of the country not altogether exposed to the mechanization of modern technology, the work in each region has a character of its own within the overall Indian form.

Rooted in their local tradition the craftsmen were mobile; sculptors in wood, ivory, or stone and painters accepted commissions that took them temporarily away from their village to a thriving monastic establishment that set up a monument to the glory of god or to a royal or princely court. While the craftsmen thus selected enriched the work, to which they were called from afar, by the style that was their own, they also took back with them new impressions that they would embody in their own work. The effects of the mobility of the professional artist and of his exposure to new patronage and demands merged in several levels with his hereditary training.

The participation in building a temple or painting the walls in a palace exacted a mastery of the highest standard as demanded by the texts and expected by the patrons. Where these standards are met, the work of art is considered as "*mārgī*," or fulfilling the tradition, and distinguished from merely local standards which vary from place to place—and by their variety add zest to their products. Classified as "*deshī*," such works belong to a specific locality and have the flavor of the specific region and its soil. The pulsation between mārgī and deshī levels links court art and folk art. It makes the lotus flower a perennial symbol of Indian art. However stylized or ritualized as abstract design, its petals stay fresh in Indian art with inexhaustible variations. The sculptor from Rajasthan who carved the top of the grinding wheel creatively formed its motion in a relief that "concentrates" the shape of wheel, sun, and lotus and chains them to the task in hand by the motifs of the serpent and the knot (Fig. 15). In this everyday object used by women, every day becomes sanctified.

Socially the artists/craftsmen—the stone and wood carvers, metalsmiths, potters, and painters—belonged to the lower level of the population, like the cooks or performers or the other members of the professions who cater to the enjoyment of life. There were sixty-four "arts" classified in ancient India. Lovemaking was one of them.

Because their standing was low on the social scale, the craftsmen were close to the tribal people and could work for them in a style conforming with their own traditions. The metal figurines in the *Dhokrā* technique—the Dhokrā was a quasi-Hinduized caste of migratory metalworkers who came to Bengal from Bihar—used by the Kutiya Konds of Orissa and other tribes correspond to and have the vitality of their own paintings although they are the work of itinerant Hindu craftsmen commissioned by the tribals.

The distinction between mārgī and deshī is blurred today by the

Fig. 15. Chakkī, Grinding Stone from Rajasthan. *19th century. Stone-carved, 52 x 22" (20 x 59 cm). Raja Dinkar Kelkar Museum, Pune.*

demands of cosmopolitan taste in the large cities that progressively estranges the artist-craftsman from his tradition, be it mārgī or deshī.

The great temples today rise as monuments of the past over a landscape that stayed productive though impoverished in its means, that stayed alive from generation to generation through the course of the years and the seasons, with the waxing and waning of the moon, with sunrise and sunset. All these moments and transitions have their response in innumerable rites and in countless shapes, many of which are not meant to last—molded in clay or made of wood or cotton—for they will be made again and again with the rites of spring or autumn, with the daily rites of evocation.

The Indian rural economy of art provides for sculptures to be made as offerings to the deity and to be left untended at the place where they were given—under a tree, near pond or river or in a grove. They accumulate, they decompose, and others take their place. It is not the form which remains and endures, but the performance which makes the form and gives it style, changing with the years as do the leaves on the trees and eventually the trees themselves, yet recognizable in its local varieties as part of the scene where the sculptures stand. In India in ancient times, the stone temples were built as works of monumental sculpture, showing forth on their walls the figure of man transmuted into the likeness of gods (ca. A.D. 500 to 1500).

Today, as in former times, there are many large towns in India, but few large temples have been built during the last centuries, under Muslim and British rule. The "Great Tradition" of architectural sculpture died a slow death. Today, as in former times, the people of India—now about 750 million—are 75 percent rural.[19] Moreover, 80 percent of the rural population worships gods other than Vishnu and Shiva, who are worshiped by Hindus in the large temples.

If outside the pale of Hindu influences, and left to themselves, people neither built temples nor made images of their gods. Their religion expresses itself directly in rites in which works of art are the indispensable and focal means of communication with the supernatural, with man's experience of the Real. The Real is sensed in the waking experience. It may be foreshadowed in dreams. It is known in trance. Trance, dream, and waking experiences are actual, though they vary in kind and degree and lie in different but interconnected planes. Tribal art gives them form.

Among the tribal people of India, the Gond, Santal, and Bhil are the most numerous groups. They are called aboriginal inasmuch as they were in India before the Aryans arrived after the middle of the second millennium B.C. However, before that time a great urban civilization, with its capital cities in the Punjab and Sind, had extended over a large part of the peninsula (second half of the second millennium B.C.). The relation of the ancestors of the present tribal people to that great urban civilization of Mohenjo-daro and Harappa is not known.

Tribal art throughout India for the last two thousand years at least must be assumed to have coexisted with traditions commanding greater means and more complex organization. The Buddhist stone railing of the stupa of Bharhut and the stupa of the saints in Sanchi, both collective monuments of sculpture of the second to first century B.C., show the work of many different hands. These stone railings with their carvings are each a symposium of styles, some of which bear affinity to tribal carvings such as those of the Gond, who to this day live not far from the sites of these ancient monuments. Although Buddhism was open to members of any group, the sculptors were not necessarily Buddhists; they came from the lower Hindu strata of ancient Indian or tribal stock. Progressing Hinduization, while dissolving many of the self-supporting and self-sufficient tribal communities, absorbed as much as it destroyed of tribal traditions, while these tribes, where they survived as solid groups, assimilated much from their suppressors, who also were their neighbors. But Hinduism from the start is an alloy of the brāhmanic tradition and the many other and older Indian traditions. Due to this long process of osmosis, tribal art in India, on the whole, lacks the stylistic certitude and perfectedness of the tribal art of Africa, Oceania, and of the American Indian. The art of the Naga, who live on the northeastern frontier of India, although relatively pure, is slighter; the tribal art of central India cruder; and that of the Bhil more heterogeneous than Congo or Melanesian creations.

Of all the tribal people of India, the small group of the Toda, who live in the Nilgiris, the Blue Hills of south India, have left what may be considered the most ancient relics (about first century A.D.). Terra cotta figurines excavated there, are, it would seem, the work of their ancestors. Some of these figurines have tribal forms, others do not essentially differ in some respects from some of the terra cottas found in Mohenjo-daro, while in certain aspects some of the Mohenjo-daro figurines can be compared with the work by village potters and women made to this day in Bengal.

The Image of the Horse

The tribal style of the Bhil, which encompasses a wide area, is shown by the figurine of the Spirit Rider. The village art of south India is represented by the sacred grove, with its many and large clay figures, mainly of horses. When the horse was brought to India from its home in inner Asia is not known. When the Aryans entered India from the north on horseback in the latter part of the second millennium B.C., the tame horse was represented in Harappan terra cotta figurines, which have been unearthed in Lothal and Rangpur. Horse riding later on was a privilege of the aristocracy, the Rajputs, the "sons of kings."

The essentially Indian tribal art form of the wide-ranging figurine of the Bhil Spirit Rider and the essentially Indian village art of the locally circumscribed cult of Aiyanār, in which the figure of the horse is exalted, show a tribal identity at the base of a variety of styles on the one hand, and an indigenous and localized style brought about by the confluence of many traditions on the other hand.

The Spirit Rider

The archetype of all the figurines of horsemen which give reality to the Nukto rite, the rite of the dead, of the Bhil has vanished from the scene. Its meaning and function, however, come to life whenever the rite is performed, and the mystery of death-in-life is once more confirmed through the figurine of the rider on his horse. It plays the leading role in this essential tribal rite of the Bhil, although the Bhil neither raise nor use horses. The equestrian figure in art and legend is generally associated with the feudal Hindu Rajputs, the northern neighbors of the Bhil.

The equestrian figure is one of the themes of art by which the tribal world and that of the feudal aristocracy are linked here on earth (Fig. 16). Over and above this, its image is a magic link between heaven and earth. This is its purpose. In this respect, the function of the equestrian figurine is not different from that of the great temples that were erected in the cities. There, the ascent to heaven was built up, stone by stone, each stone carved with an image appropriate to its position in the entire edifice, piled high so that step by step the architectural ritual of the ascent became the monument, the temple. The architectural ritual is put into words in the ancient texts of that science. The oral tradition of the tribal Bhil to this day verifies step by step the journey of the soul that has the Spirit Rider for its acting support.

The tribe of the Bhil, the "sons of the forest," lives in western India, from the Aravalli Mountains in Rajasthan to the Vindhya range. It is in and near this region that in the course of the last two thousand years the Buddhist cave temples and monasteries of Ajanta were cut out of the rocks, the Jains built the marble temples at Mount

Abu, and many Hindu shrines have borne witness to the experience of the sacred. The Bhil were hunters, fishermen, and food gatherers—they have learned animal husbandry from their neighbors, the Gujār—and they are agriculturists. Although centered in Rajasthan (Mewār), Gujarat, and Khandesh, they also live in loosely connected groups in the mountains and the less readily accessible parts of Sind (in Pakistan), Kutch, and Rajasthan in the northwest and in the state of Andhra Pradesh in the southeast. A small group of them is found as far to the northeast as Bengal. Their original language is lost; they form a psychological complex without linguistic, physiognomic, economic, or cultural unity. Their spirituality is their own and forms a bond that holds them together.

Formerly they ruled over their own country. This was prior to the arrival of the Rajputs. The Rajputs, the "sons of kings," invaded the country, subsequently Rajasthan, in about the sixth century A.D. They became kshatriyas, the nobility *par excellence* of India.

The Rajputs are horse owners and riders. The Bhil use the image of the horseman; it is that of a Spirit Rider, the Gothriz Purvez, the ancestor of the clan. On it is focused the solidarity of the clan; it redeems the dead and liberates the living from the fear of death and the despair of loneliness. Moreover, the Bhil commemorate their fallen heroes, killed in a fight or cattle raid, by setting up stone memorial slabs carved in low relief with an equestrian figure; whereas memorial stones set up for their dead by others, the Rajputs in particular, frequently have a standing figure in front view. The Bhil confer on their ancestors the nobility of the horseman, whereas the Rajputs do not particularly stress the equestrian form of their dead. From the hymns of the Rig Veda (Rig Veda 1.163.2), which was produced in the last part of the second millennium B.C., the group of horse and rider is vested with sacredness. Indra, the Creator God, rode the horse for the first time. Later tradition knows the Sun God as rider and the horse itself as fire in all its aspects, on earth and in heaven, the sun on high and the spark of life.

The Bhil ritual for the dead is celebrated in front of the entrance of the house of the deceased. From above its lintel a twelve-runged bamboo ladder is suspended and subsequently also a long string with an arrow—the Bhil were primarily hunters—attached to it. This man-made setting and its paraphernalia contrast with the sacred grove, the central sanctuary of every Bhil settlement. There, an unhewn stone or stones are the symbols of deity. In the cult of the dead, however, man is the symbol. The anthropomorphic image and representation, which are here those of the horseman, are linked with the cult of the dead. Another object required for the great Nukto rite, the rite of the dead,

Fig. 16. Equestrian Figure. *18th century. Brass, 4³/₄ x 4¹/₄ x 1¹/₄" (11¹/₂ x 10¹/₂ x 3¹/₂ cm). Rajasthan.*

is the figurine of a cow. These figurines are made of the copper anklets of the widow of the deceased. The material itself of the figurines has magical virtue; it takes part in the ritual and undergoes a spiritual alchemy.

The Gothriz Purvez is placed on an altar, the cow on a metal tray. The long string leads to the altar of the Gothriz Purvez and thence to the cow. Now the scene is set. The main actors are the *rawal*, the master of ceremonies, the *barwo*, the magician, and the *waha*, the priest. The waha, who acts as a Brāhman or priest, is a male child from the clan of the dead person.

The preparation for the Nukto rite begins when the rawal sings to the dying man at the first ghanto, corresponding to the first rung of the ladder: "Alone go, brother, to Bhagavān (the Supreme God) through the seven depths." And at the third ghanto, the rawal speaks over the dead body: "Come, quite alone." And at the fifth ghanto, it is the spirit (*jīva*) who speaks: "I am alone, brother, I am alone." The rungs of the bamboo ladder, which the rawal had hung from the doorframe, represent the twelve stations of the mountain with their obstacles which the jīva, the spirit, has to climb before it is purified and reaches Bhagavān.

The Bhil distinguish between the body, the psychic elements or the ghost (*bhūta*) and shadow, and the spirit of man. They separate at death. The body is cremated; a heap of stones is piled up under a tree. There the bhūta is appeased in the first three days of the rites, after the death of the body. On the fourth day, the Nukto rites of three days begin. It is then that the rawal ties the string on the wooden crossbar above the entrance. When the jīva has attained the seventh rung, the stones are scattered; there is now no resting place on earth for any part of the man who died. The spirit rises from one rung of tests and judgment to the next, overcoming the obstacles of each rung. The spirit is purified during the ascent. In the night, when the spirit has passed the tenth and eleventh rungs and has been judged in the twelve courts, it goes to Bhagavān. The rawal has sprinkled the cow with milk to make the spirit pure and white. When the spirit has completed its ascent, during the first Nukto rite, on the fourth day after death, the twelve rungs of the ladder are destroyed, the spirit descends along the string into the arrow, the rawal having poured water three times over the cow. By these rites, the spirit is further purified. The spirit now enters the equestrian figurine and the cow and overcomes the barwo, who, meanwhile having undergone the necessary preparations, is in a trance. The spirit makes the barwo select the waha, a young boy from the clan of the dead, who is now consecrated. The waha is the Gothriz Purvez; he is possessed by the spirit and is given the same name as the rider figurine on the horse who is the Gothriz Purvez, the ancestor of the clan, the liberated spirit of the man who had died. The waha, trembling in his trance, holds the tablet with the figurine of the cow, while the rawal sings for the *khatariz* (kshatriya), the hero, the spirit.

When the figurine of the cow, held by the trembling waha, has itself ceased to tremble, it is taken in procession to the tree where the stones were collected and then were scattered. The figurine of the cow is buried.

The rawal tears the string on which the spirit has descended. The waha is no longer possessed by the spirit. The purified spirit has been accepted in the clan of the ancestors. It dwells with Bhagavān, in the beyond. The Nukto rite has been completed. A meal and mask dance follow.

Aiyanār

In south India, in almost every Tamil village there is a shrine of Aiyanār. Often a large, rough stone without any carving is set up under a tree. It stands for the presence of Aiyanār. Such a stone setting belongs to tribal tradition. But Aiyanār is a deity of the Brāhmans and his worshipers are Dravidian villagers. Generally his sanctuary is on the banks of a pond. Its waters fertilize the fields that he protects. In some of his sanctuaries, Aiyanār is represented in human shape, a kingly figure riding a horse or an elephant. Horses are offered to him, large terra cotta horses, so that he does not lack a mount during the watches of the night when he rides around the village and looks after its safety. He rides with his retinue of heroes— and demons. Two horses at least must be offered to Aiyanār each year. The second is for Karuppan, the Dark God, the demon who accompanies him. Over the years, the horses accumulate in the sacred groves. Up to five hundred such large clay horses (up to ten feet or more) may be ready in one sanctuary for the nocturnal rides (Fig. 17). New horses are set up, while the old and broken ones are left to decay and return to the earth of which they were made. Under the image of Aiyanār a stone linga, the phallic symbol of Shiva's creativeness, is buried. The seed of Shiva, from which Aiyanār was born, it is said, fell near the banks of the waters.

The sacred lives integrally in Aiyanār's sanctuaries, in the waters near by and in the soil, in the trees that enshrine the multitude of clay horses in their upright splendor and in their decay where, fallen to the ground, they are left to return to the earth whose mystery emanates from the total setting and pervades the heterogeneous but utterly consistent legend of Aiyanār. These open-air south Indian village sanctu-

Fig. 17. A village sanctuary of Aiyanār. Velankulattur (Paramagudi).

aries are replete with a living art and the living knowledge of the underlying myth whose components and ritual range from Brāhmanic to tribal tradition.

Aiyanār, the Lord, is the son of the two great Hindu gods: Shiva, the ascetic Creator-Destroyer; and Vishnu, the Preserver. In order to arouse Shiva, Vishnu assumed the shape of a wonderfully beautiful girl called Mohinī, or Delusion. She excited Shiva, and he let his seed fall near the waters. From it, Aiyanār, the son of Shiva and Vishnu, was born. A king, while hunting, found the beautiful infant lying on the ground, crying, but his face radiant with a thousand suns.

The main sanctuary of Aiyanār, the Lord, is in the thickly wooded Shabari hills in Kerala near the western coast of south India. There the Lord protects man from evil spirits and endows him with knowledge that leads to salvation. But in the sanctuary of Erumeli in Kerala, Aiyanār is worshiped in the form of a hunter. His devotees dance wildly when they worship the Lord of this world of delusion, might, and fear.

Neither the wisdom aspect nor the orgiastic one are overtly part of the divinity of Aiyanār in the eastern, Tamil part of south India (he is not known north of the Godavari River), but the mystery of his birth from the two great Hindu gods passed on to the potency of the waters and the earth of any particular locality where Aiyanār is worshiped. While he is the same everywhere, each time it is a different Aiyanār who is worshiped.

The Lord, Aiyanār, the guardian of the land, has his generals and lieutenants. They are heroes, that is, they are the souls of those who died in battle. They are joined by the host of demons, foremost Karuppan, the Dark God, who is all that Aiyanār is not. He is the adversary to whom blood sacrifices are due. Aiyanār is worshiped with flowers and fruits. The dark power within Aiyanār, the Hunter, has been embodied in Karuppan, his alter ego, the demon as protector. Together they are worshiped by the officiating priest, who also is the maker of their images, the village potter. During worship he becomes possessed by Karuppan, the Dark God, the alter ego of Aiyanār. Himself potter and priest, he molds the clay horses, impressing the clay with tensions experienced in shamanistic possession. The clay itself is taken from a ground of sacred fertility. It holds the linga of Shiva and the seed from which Aiyanār has sprung. Aiyanār, the Lord, scion of the two great Hindu gods, King of Demons, synthesis of deity experienced on the many levels of India's religious structure, depends on the clay horses offered to him for his rides. Their power is vested in the soil from which they are made. It does not extend beyond the Tamil village and its indigenous art.

The Spirit Riders of the Bhil, Aiyanār with his equestrian retinue of heroes and demons, each have their own locale, myths, and rites. The form of the sculptures is their visual equivalent and residue. Less rich in myth and rites are the traditions of the Spirit Riders who guard the villages all over India and whose equestrian images and votive horses are made by the village potters in basic, primary shapes. They all ride without stirrups, on saddled or unsaddled horses. Where no rider is figured plastically, the living human medium in his frenzy may symbolically mount a clay horse by putting his toes on it.

The horse is one of the main themes in the tribal and rural art of India. It rode deep into the interior of the country, carrying the liberated spirit and its own nobility, power, and fertility. It brings wish fulfillment to the poor and the suppressed. It has vivified the creative imagination of village potters and tribal craftsmen and is an outpost of their innumerable styles. Known in India from the remote past, once more, carrying its Aryan rider, it had entered India from on high, from the north, across the mountains and the social and ethnic strata of the country.

The figure of the horse in the art of tribal and rural India retained its basic shape, particularly in the small terra cotta images, alongside a form that has become more complex by assimilating to its own simplicity the naturalism that was part of the Great Tradition of Indian sculpture, as in the Tamil village horses, or by raising the little images of the Spirit Rider to expressive, sensitive, stylistically variegated emblems of the Bhil clans and the people of tribal and rural India.

The cow, sacred to the Hindus, and particularly the bull in the shape of Nandī, were given their immortal form in the various schools of sculpture of the Great Tradition. Thence their grandiose, weighty volumes descended, simplified, and carved in stone or wood, to the level of folk art. They remain distinct from the primary geometry of the tribal-village art forms.

In ancient times, in the second millennium B.C., the basic form of the bull, impetuously modeled, coexisted with its naturalistic shape, in Mohenjo-daro. In a primary shape, the buffalo was found also in the ancient tombs of the Nilgiris of south India.

Though softened at times by descriptive naturalism, animal sculpture retained its basic, seemingly timeless cast. Ram, boar, and elephant are created as if nourished on the same peaceful pasture.

The tribal-village continuum of rural India extends, even today, into the towns as it must have at any other time. In the Harappan cities of prehistoric antiquity, terra cotta figurines abounded. They have tubular shapes or conical stumps for limbs, cylindrical or flattened bodies, faces pinched so that pellets for eyes can be affixed on either side of the nose. Similar figurines are made today by the potters or the women of the village. According to the use that will be made of the clay figurines, they will be toys or, if consecrated, ritual objects. While some of the figurines are precise and subtle in proportions and contour, others are sketchy or less competent in execution. But there are, besides these simple, basic types, naturalistically modeled figurines, and others whose faces are molded. Many layers and phases of art, tribal or urban, left their residues in these most ancient towns of the subcontinent, as they did subsequently in other cities.

Figures on the Wall

Although the women's art of drawing abstract ritual patterns on the floor spread over India in all directions, it did not extend to tribal India. There, domestic ritual painting is practiced almost entirely by men, with few exceptions. The wall paintings of these non-Aryan, non-Dravidian tribal people—the Saoras of Orissa, the Warlis of Gujarat and the Deccan, the Gonds and Pardhans of Central India, the Bhils of Gujarat, the Konds of Orissa—irrespective of their ethnic roots have one thing in common. They are pictographs full of the figures of man, animal, tree, building, and vehicle. Among the Saoras all of these are seen in dreams.[20] The tribal artist sees in a dream the picture he is about to paint. Each painting has a definite purpose—to increase the fertility of the crops, to honor the dead, or, in case of calamity, to assuage, praise, and flatter the god or ghost whom the householder, the painter of the picture, fears to have offended. The magician-priest diagnoses the trouble and advises the householder to paint an appropriate picture, which he will see in his dream. Should the householder fail to see the picture in his dream, he will delegate the painting of it to an experienced painter who will spend the night before the wall to be painted after having made an offering to the deity concerned. Or, the magician-priest himself may paint the required picture of the other world of the gods, ghosts, and the dead. In the morning after the first sketch is made, the priest will call upon the deity in whose honor the painting is made. The spirit comes to him and makes his suggestions.

The priest-magician has close contacts with the spirit world. Its denizens are pleased by the work of the painter, be he the householder, a more experienced painter, or the magician-priest himself. The subject of the painting is the spirit world seen in the dream and trance, with its events as they relate to the particular situation of the dreamer. He sees the spirit world. It extends suspended in his dreaming mind and he makes this other world visible: when awake from his

Fig. 18. A Saora pictograph of the hill abode of the god Borongsum. The drawing is from the village of Avangulu, Ganjam District, Orissa. *Height, 20 inches.*

dream he paints it on the wall of his house. By the act of painting he establishes the reality of the other world and by doing so he frees himself from guilt and worry. With the help of the magician-priest he can identify the figures his dreaming self had seen in that other world.

Artistic creation for the tribal painter is divided in two stages, the vision in the dream and the act of painting when fully awake. Before the painter begins his work, offerings are made to the deity or ghost. The painter fasts from the morning of the day of his work until it is completed. Once it has served its purpose, the picture is meant to stay on the wall, fufilling the role of a domestic shrine. Before beginning his work the painter addresses himself to the deity: "I have been told to make you a house." He starts his painting by depicting the residence of the deity, generally a square or rectangular shape that hovers in the picture occupying a central position, though not the exact center (Fig. 18).[21] The mansion of the deity is delimited by strong framing lines, in some cases elaborated like lace work. Within, the mansion in some paintings is ordered in rectilinear subdivisions, each a compartment of its own; meticulously aligned figures fill its extent in horizontal rows. Outside the palace float the precisely defined figures of men and animals, their gender not indicated. Incidental trees swarm with monkeys; horses and elephants with and without riders walk in procession; tigers, stags, and lizards, peacocks and other birds, but also the sun, moon, and stars float in free symmetry all around the mansion (Fig. 19). Men are depicted frontally, animals in profile, objects in whatever view they demand to be recognizable; all the figures convey motion—this is their privilege as spirit figures. Their size is determined as the eye demands, without reference either to proportion as it exists in the world of man or to the importance of the figures as it is in traditional Indian art.

The spirit world bristles with constant movement in rows of dancers or retainers of the god or spirit, while others are busy in their respective work. Whether riding on horseback or elephant or in trains and cars, as in some of the paintings, the figures have the same alert elation, for the deity or ghost of the mansion displays his wealth in the number of his retainers and visitors and in the liveliness of his world. To satisfy the god or ghost whom, according to the diagnosis of the priest-magician, the painter must have neglected in his respect or otherwise offended, the artist paints the spirit world in affluent splendor. Processions of dancers, retainers, sword bearers, and horsemen are interspersed with single figures and various groups, some seated at ease outside the mansion. They are sahibs, British officials, visitors; their elegance is nonchalant as they sit on high-backed chairs, smoking and reading. In other paintings, groups of two or three

Fig. 19. A Saora pictograph of the hill abode of the god Benasum. This drawing is also from the village of Avangulu, Ganjam District, Orissa. *Height, 24 inches.*

267

include a four-armed, two-headed, four-legged figure, a scene of copulating spirits, trains, a bicycle rider, or planes in motion. Integrated in its form and rendered in his own style by the individual painter, the spirit world is analogous to this world with the difference that it is not subject to gravity. Spirits have no bulk. They are seen in dreams and projected on the wall by the tribal pictographer.

The figures in the paintings of the Saoras—pre-eminent in the tribal art of India—on the mud walls of their houses are painted with a brush made of a twig, its tip splayed; the medium generally is rice paste applied in lines and solid areas in white on an ochre-red ground. The figures precipitated on this ground and painted there are not just the *likeness* of those of the other world. They *are* those figures; they exist by having been painted. Form is their world, the "other world," the reality of art.

Domestic ritual art, whether abstract and practiced by Hindu women on the mud floor or figurative and practiced by tribal men on the mud walls of their houses, has a life span of hundreds or thousands of years. Today contemporary means of communication and mechanization leave little scope for its practice. Is it possible that tribal art survives when no longer performed as a ritual, when the tradition of which it is the form is on the wane, and when the individual genius of one or the other tribal painter is its only repository? Jivya Soma, a Warli painter, substituting mud and cow dung primed paper for the mud walls of his house, imbued the themes of Warli paintings with a finesse and alertness of his own (Figs. 20, 21). In the Warli pictographs, the firm pivot of the figure, the denizen of the spirit world consisted, as in all tribal paintings, of one triangle only or of two triangles, the upper one with its point down, meeting the point of the lower triangle. After triangles were drawn, the limbs were added, their long thin lines and sharp angles conveying energy, having direction, and suggesting movement. In Jivya Soma's drawings, the two triangles are not always in vertical position. Like the limbs of the figures, the triangles are placed at angles, so that the bodies are flexed at the waist and can assume any posture. Jivya Soma's figures bend and move with superb freedom. In similar freedom of movement the trees and shrubs in his paintings throw forth miraculous branches of dazzling inventiveness. Tribal art, emerging from its ritual context, presents figures of the other world as it flares up in the creation of a remarkable artist. Jivya Soma lately has placed the whole tradition of Warli ritual art that had nourished his own unrivaled creativity in the service of narrative, of Warli myths and legends, substituting the reality of the other world with his illustrated fairy tale.

Fig. 20. Detail of a painting entitled "Day of Rejoicing" by Jivya Soma.

Fig. 21. A cluster pictograph by Jivya Soma.

Biographies

Pria Devi

Miss Pria Devi, a graduate of Vassar College, is well known in India for her creative writings in English. She has written two volumes of poetry and has published several critiques on major Indian artists. She currently is studying Sanskrit in Varanasi, and is working on translations of the works of Abhinavagupta (c. 1000 A.D.), who was a renowned Kashmiri Shaiva philosopher and critic of poetry and drama.

Nazir Jairazbhoy

Dr. Nazir Jairazbhoy was educated in India, England, and the United States and is an ethnomusicologist in the Department of Music at the University of California, Los Angeles. He is a past president of the Society for Ethnomusicology, and he has conducted 15 research trips to India and Pakistan between 1954 and 1985. He has been associate professor of music at the University of Windsor (Ontario) and lecturer of Indian music at the School of Oriental and African Studies (London). He also has been a visiting lecturer at the Universities of Washington, Illinois, and Michigan, and at Dartington College of Arts (South Devon, England). He has worked with Smithsonian scholars on several projects in the past and currently is finishing a film and monograph on the culture of *kathputlī* (marionette) puppeteers of Rajasthan, India, with the Smithsonian's Office of Folklife Programs. He is the author of numerous scholarly articles and the book, *Ragas of North Indian Music: Their Structure and Evolution*. He has also written, directed, and edited two videotapes entitled *Folk Performers of India* and *Folk Musicians of Rajasthan*.

Pupul Jayakar

Mrs. Pupul Jayakar is chairman of the Indian Advisory Committee for the Festival of India. She is a pioneer in the field of rural arts and design and has held many important positions in the Government of India. Her past chairmanships include those of The Handicrafts and Handlooms Exports Corporation of India Ltd., the All India Handicrafts Board, the Central Cottage Industries Corporation, and the Governing Body of the National Institute of Design, Ahmedabad. She was given India's prestigious Padma Bhushan award in 1967 for her achievements in the field of handloom development. In addition, to numerous scholarly articles and a volume of short stories, Mrs. Jayakar is the author of the book, *Earthen Drum: An Introduction to the Ritual Arts of Rural India*.

Sudhir Kakar

Dr. Sudhir Kakar is an internationally noted psychoanalyst and a senior fellow at the Centre for the Study of Developing Societies in Delhi. He has combined degrees in engineering, economics, and political economy from universities in India, West Germany, and Austria with postgraduate work at West Germany's Sigmund Freud Institute. He has been a lecturer at Harvard University and a visiting professor of behavioral sciences at the Universities of Frankfurt and Vienna. Until the fall of 1983, he was chairman of the Department of Humanities and Social Sciences and taught at the Institute of Technology in New Delhi. Most recently, he has been a research fellow at the Institute for Advanced Study, Princeton University. His many publications include *The Inner World: A Psychoanalytic Study of Childhood and Society in India*, *Identity and Adulthood*, and *Shamans, Mystics, and Doctors*.

Stella Kramrisch

Dr. Stella Kramrisch is the foremost interpreter of Indian art and its religious contexts. Her book, *The Hindu Temple*, offers a seminal approach to the architecture and visual arts of India. During her sixty-year career as a creative scholar, teacher, museum curator, and editor, she has been a dominant force in shaping European, American, and Asian notions of Indian culture. Her early life and education were spent in Vienna before World War I. From 1923 to 1950, she taught at Calcutta University. Since 1950, she has taught at the University of Pennsylvania and at the Institute of Fine Arts at New York University, and served as curator of Indian Art at the Philadelphia Museum of Art. During these years, she has focused her energies on a series of major exhibitions and textual studies, culminating in the exhibition, *Manifestations of Shiva*, and in her book, *The Presence of Shiva*. In January 1982, Dr. Kramrisch was awarded the Government of India's high honor of Padma Bhushan in recognition of her scholarship and devotion to Indian art. Dr. Kramrisch has written many provocative books and more than 200 articles and reviews, primarily on Indian art.

Richard Kurin

Dr. Richard Kurin is a University of Chicago-educated anthropologist on the faculty of Southern Illinois University at Carbondale. He is currently on leave to the Smithsonian Institution to consult and coordinate several of its Festival of India programs. A former Fulbright-Hays, Social Science Research Council, and National Endowment for the Humanities Fellow, he has conducted intensive field research in rural and urban India and Pakistan. His publications on the family, social structure, folk knowledge, and cultural change have appeared in several books and such journals as *Natural History*, *Human Organization*, *The Journal of Asian Studies*, *Asian Survey*, *Middle East Studies*, and *Contributions to Indian Sociology*.

Wendy Doniger O'Flaherty

Dr. Wendy Doniger O'Flaherty was born in New York in 1940 and trained as a dancer under George Balanchine and Martha Graham before beginning the study of Sanskrit at Radcliffe College in 1958. She holds doctoral degrees in Indian studies from Harvard and Oxford Universities, and is now Professor of the History of Religions and Indian Studies and a member of the Committee on Social Thought at the University of Chicago. Her publications include *Dreams, Illusion and Other Realities*, *Women, Androgynes and Other Mythical Beasts*, *Asceticism and Eroticism in the Mythology of Siva*, *The Origins of Evil in Hindu Mythology*, *Tales of Sex and Violence: Folklore, Sacrifice and Danger in the Jaiminiya Brahmana*, *Hindu Myths*, an edited volume, *Karma and Rebirth in Classical Indian Traditions*, and a translation of the *Rig Veda*, as well as numerous articles on Indian religion and mythology.

Rajeev Sethi

Mr. Rajeev Sethi is a member of the Indian Advisory Committee for the Festival of India. He is one of India's leading designers and has directed numerous projects in India, Europe, Britain, and North America as well as for the United Nations. During the past several years, Mr. Sethi also has been involved in comprehensive rural development schemes for the preservation of cultural heritage. He is the designer and curator for three Smithsonian exhibitions organized especially for the Festival of India: *Aditi—A Celebration of Life* at the National Museum of Natural History (June 4 to July 28, 1985), a traditional *Melā* (an Indian fair) at the annual Festival of American Folklife on the National Mall (June 26 to July 7, 1985), and *The Golden Eye* at the Cooper-Hewitt Museum (November 5, 1985 to January 19, 1986).

Notes and Bibliographies

Aditi— A Celebration
of Life
Pria Devi and
Richard Kurin

Notes

The authors are grateful to Saleem Kidwai, Inder Dan Detha, and Prema Srinivasan for providing specific material included in the text on Muslim, Rajasthani, and Tamil culture, respectively.

1. Adapted from Ralph T. H. Griffith, ed. and trans., *Hymns of the Rigveda*, 3rd ed. (Benares: E.J. Lazarus, 1920), v. 1, p. 115.

2. This and other unattributed poetic passages in the essay for *Aditi* by Pria Devi.

3. Adapted from Griffith, *op. cit.*, p. 416, fn.

4. Bengali song recorded by and trans. Pria Devi.

5. Maharathi verse recorded by M. N. Deshpande, trans. Pria Devi.

6. Bengali verse recorded by Sukanta Basu, trans. Pria Devi.

7. A. K. Ramanujan, trans., *The Interior Landscape: Love Poems from a Classical Tamil Anthology* (Bloomington: Indiana University Press, 1967), p. 62.

8. *ibid.*, p. 48.

9. Adapted from Thakur Ramsinha, Suryakaran Parik and Narottamdas Swami, *Rajasthan ke Lokgit* [1939], trans. L. Winifred Bryce and R.P. Dhundale. *Women's Folksongs of Rajputana* (Delhi: Ministry of Information and Broadcasting, 1964), p. 69.

10. *ibid.*, p. 68.

11. *ibid.*, p. 74-75.

12. Verrier Elwin, *The Muria and their Ghotul* (London: Oxford University Press, 1947), p. 106.

13. Adapted from Ralph T.H. Griffith, ed. and trans., *The Hymns of the Atharva-veda*, 3rd ed. (Varanasi: Khelari Lal, 1962), v.2, p. 182.

14. Adapted from Oscar Lewis, *Village Life in Northern India* (Urbana: University of Illinois Press, 1958), p. 181.

15. Adapted from Chandramani Singh, *Marriage Songs from Bhojpuri Region* (Jaipur: Champa Lal Ranka, 1979), p. 87.

16. Mohammed M. Pickthall, trans., *The Glorious Koran* (New York: Mentor, 1953), p. 242.

17. Rajasthani folksong recorded by Dan Detha, trans. Pria Devi.

18. Rajasthani folksong recorded by Inder Dan Detha, trans. Pria Devi.

19. S. Radhakrishnan, *The Principal Upanisads* (London: George Allen and Unwin, 1953), p. 522.

20. *The Holy Bible*, trans. from the Latin Vulgate, Douay [1609] (Baltimore: John Murphy, 1899), p. 701.

21. Rajasthani folksong, recorded by Inder Dan Detha, trans. Pria Devi.

22. Tamil song recorded by Dr. Anandlakshmy, trans. Pria Devi.

23. Thakur Ramsinha Bryce, *op. cit.*, p. 142.

24. Adapted from Kannada song recorded by Dr. Anandlakshmy, trans. Pria Devi.

25. *ibid.*

26. Occhavlal Mohanlal Shah, ed., *Vallabhusudha* (Dohad Lalchand Shah, 1959).

27. Adapted from S. Radhakrishnan, ed., *The Dhammapada* (London: Oxford University Press, 1950), p. 99.

28. Adapted from Maria C. Byrski, *Concept of Ancient Indian Theatre* (New Delhi: Mushiram Manoharlal, 1974), p. 152.

29. Adapted from (Raj: Bali) Pandey, *Hindu Samskaras: Socio-Religious Study of the Hindu Sacraments* (Delhi: Motilal Banarsidass, 1969), p. 109

The Role of Myth in
the Indian Life Cycle
Wendy Doniger O'Flaherty

Notes

1. G. Morris Carstairs, *The Twice-Born* (Bloomington: Indiana University, 1958), 156-167; Wendy Doniger O'Flaherty, *Women, Androgynes, and Other Mythical Beasts* (Chicago: University of Chicago Press, 1980), 114-15.

2. Paul Courtright, *Ganeśa: Lord of Obstacles, Lord of Beginnings* (Oxford: Oxford University Press, 1985).

3. Wendy Doniger O'Flaherty, *Hindu Myths: A Sourcebook, Translated from Sanskrit* (Harmondsworth, England: Penguin, 1975), 261-69.

4. This and all other translated quotations from the Rig Veda are from Wendy Doniger O'Flaherty, *The Rig Veda: An Anthology* (Harmondsworth, England: Penguin, 1981).

5. O'Flaherty, *Women, Androgynes, and Other Mythical Beasts*.

6. Manisha Roy, *Bengali Women* (Chicago: University of Chicago Press, 1972), 41-42.

7. Wendy Doniger O'Flaherty, *Asceticism and Eroticism in the Mythology of Siva* (Oxford: Oxford University Press, 1973; reprinted as *Siva: The Erotic Ascetic*, 1981), 213-220.

8. Ibid., 221-23.

9. Ibid., 226-33.

10. O'Flaherty, *Hindu Myths*, 197-205; O'Flaherty, *Women, Androgynes, and Other Mythical Beasts*, 79-80.

11. John Stratton Hawley, *At Play with Krishna. Pilgrimage Dramas from Brindavan* (Princeton: Princeton University Press, 1981).

12. David Haberman, "Imitating the Masters: Problems in Incongruency," *Journal of the American Academy of Religion* (March 1985).

13. Alan Dundes, "The Hero Pattern and the Life of Jesus," in *Essays in Folkloristics* (Meerut, India: The Folklore Institute, 1978), 223-62.

14. Wendy Doniger O'Flaherty, *Karma and Rebirth in Classical Indian Traditions* (Berkeley and Los Angeles: University of California Press, 1980) 5-9.

15. Ibid., 21.

16. Ibid., 212-13.

17. Wendy Doniger O'Flaherty, "Inside and Outside the Mouth of God: The Boundary between Myth and Reality," *Daedalus* (Spring 1980): 119.

18. Ibid., 120.

Bibliography

Carstairs, G. Morris. 1958. *The Twice-born*. Indiana University Press.

Courtright, Paul. 1985. *Ganeśa: Lord of Obstacles, Lord of Beginnings*. Oxford University Press.

Dundes, Alan. 1978. "The Hero Pattern and the Life of Jesus." In *Essays in Folkloristics*, by Alan Dundes. Meerut (Folklore Institute), India, Pp. 223-62.

Haberman, David. 1985. "Acting as a Way of Salvation: Raganugabhakti Sadhana." *Journal of the American Academy of Religion*.

Hawley, John Stratton. 1981. *At Play with Krishna. Pilgrimage Dramas from Brindavan*. Princeton University Press. 1983. *Krishna, The Butter Thief*. Princeton University Press.

O'Flaherty, Wendy Doniger. 1973. *Asceticism and Eroticism in the Mythology of Shiva*. Oxford University Press. (Reprinted, 1981, as *Shiva: The Erotic Ascetic*).

1975. *Hindu Myths: A Sourcebook, translated from the Sanskrit*. Penguin (Harmondsworth).

1980a. *Women, Androgynes, and Other Mythical Beasts*. The University of Chicago Press.

1980b. *Karma and Rebirth in Classical Indian Traditions*.

1980c. "Inside and Outside the Mouth of God: The Boundary between Myth and Reality." *Daedalus* (Spring, 1980). Pp. 93-125.

1981. *The Rig Veda: An Anthology*. Penguin (Harmondsworth).

1984. *Dreams, Illusion, and Other Realities*. The University of Chicago Press.

1985. *Tales of Sex and Violence: Folklore, Sacrifice, and Danger in the Jaiminiya Brahmana*. The University of Chicago Press.

Roy, Manisha. 1972. *Bengali Women*. The University of Chicago Press.

The Child in India
Sudhir Kakar

Notes

1) See D.D. Kosambi, *The Culture and Civilization of Ancient India in Historical Outline* (*New Delhi: Vikas, 1970*), 16.

2) *Adi Parva*, tr. M.M. Dutta, vol. 1 of *The Mahabharata* Calcutta: Oriental Publishing Co. (n.d.) 107-8.

3) *Ibid.*, 510.

4) Kālidāsa, *Raghuvamsha*, 3: 45-6 (my translation).

5) See, for example, M. Cormack, *The Hindu Woman*, (Bombay: Asia Publishing House, 1961) p. 11; S.C. Dube, *Indian Village*, (New York: Harper and Row, 1967) 148-9; T.N. Madan, *Family and Kinship* (Bombay: Asia Publishing House, 1965) 77; L. Minturn and J.T. Hitchcock, "The Rajputs of Khalapur, India", in *Six Cultures: Studies of Child-rearing*, ed. B.B. Whiting (New York: John Wiley, 1963) 307-8. See also, William J. Goode, *World Revolution and Family Patterns*, (New York: The Free press, 1963) 235-6; and D.G. Mandelbaum, *Society in India*, vol. 1 (Berkeley: University of California Press, 1970) 120. Cases of post-partum depression, for example, are much more commonly reported among mothers who give birth to a daughter than among those who have a son. See M.R. Gaitonde, "Cross-Cultural Study of the Psychiatric Syndromes in Out-Patient Clinics in Bombay, India, and Topeka, Kansas", *International Journal of Social Psychiatry*, 4 (1958):103.

6) Oscar Lewis, *Village Life in Northern India* (New York:Vintage Books,1958)195.

7) Irawati Karve, *Kinship Organization in India* (Bombay: Asia Publishing House, 1968) 206.

8) *The Laws of Manu* G. Buhler (Oxford: Clarendon Press, 1886) 114.

9) *Ibid.*, IV, 179.

10 *Ibid.*, IV, 282-3

11) *Ibid.*, VIII, 299-300; IX, 230.

12) Richard B. Lyman Jr., "Barbarism and Religion: Late Roman and Early Medieval Childhood," in *The History of Childhood*, ed. L. de Mause (New York: Harper Torchbooks, 1975) 84.

13) *Caraka Samhita* (Delhi: Motilal Banarsidass, 1975), Sarira 8:96.

14) *Susruta Samhita*, Sarira 10:38.

15) Srinivas Sharma, *Adhunik Hindi Kavya Vatsalya Rasa* quoted in C. Rawat, *Sur Sahitya*, (Mathura: Jawahar Pustakalaya, 1967) 230.

16) Surdas, *Sursagarsar*, D. Verma (Allahabad: Shitya Bhawan, 1972) 59 (my translation).

17) Goswami Tulsidas, *Kavitavali* R.P. Tripathi (Allahabad: Bharati Niketan, n.d.) 3 (my translation).

18) In this connection, see the various contributions in de Mause's *The History of Childhood*, especially the review essay "The Evolution of Childhood," 1-73.

19) For a textual description of the contents of the *samskāras* see Raj B. Pandey, *Hindu Samskaras*, (Delhi: Motilal Banarsidass, 1969).

20) For a more detailed discussion see "Mothers and Infants," chap. 3 in Sudhir Kakar, *The Inner World: A Psychoanalytic Study of Childhood and Society in India* (New York and Delhi: Oxford University Press, 1978).

21) See R. Sankrantyan and D.K. Upadhyaya, eds. *Hindi Sahitya ka Vrihat Itihas*, vol. 16, part 3 (Kashi: Nagaripracharni Sabha, n.d.) 111.

22) Dube, *op. cit.*, 149.

23) S. Anandalakshmi, "Socialization for Competence: A Study of Children in Four Craft Communities" (unpublished manuscript, Lady Irvin College, Delhi).

24) See D.M. Bassa, "From the Traditional to the Modern: Some Observations on Changes in Indian Child-Rearing and Parental Attitudes" in *The Child in his Family: Children and their Parents in a Changing World*, ed. E.J. Anthony and C. Chiland (New York: J. Wiley, 1978) 333-44, and Champa Aphale, *Growing Up in an Urban Complex* (New Delhi: National, 1976).

25) P.V. Kare, *History of Dharamsastra*, vol. 2, part 1, (Poona: Bhandarkar Oriental Research Institute, 1933) 180.

Performance, Music, and the Child

Nazir A. Jairazbhoy

References Cited

Berland, Joseph C. *No Five Fingers Are Alike*. Cambridge, Mass.: Harvard University Press, 1982.

Bharata-Muni. *The Natyasastra*, vols. I and II. Translated by Manmohan Ghosh. Calcutta: The Asiatic Society of Bengal, 1951, 1961.

Panini. *Astaadhyayi*. Edited and translated by O. Böhtlingk. Leipzig: 1887.

Russell, R.V. and Hiralal. *The Tribes and Castes of the Central Provinces of India*. 4 Volumes. London: Macmillan and Co, 1916.

Schechner, Richard. *Essays on Performance Theory 1970-1976*. New York: Drama Book Specialist, 1977.

Suggested Further Reading

Basham, A.L. *The Wonder That Was India*. New York: Grove Press, 1959.

Berland, Joseph C. *No Five Fingers Are Alike*. Cambridge, Mass.: Harvard University Press, 1982.

Bhavnani, Enakshi. *The Dance in India*, Bombay: D.B. Taraporevala Sons & Co. Pvt. Ltd., 1965.

Chettiar, S.M.L. Lakshmanan. *Folklore of Tamil Nadu*. Delhi: Thomson Press, 1973.

Durga, S.A.K. *The Opera in South India*. Delhi: B.R. Publishing, 1979.

Gargi, Balwant. *Folk Theater of India*. Seattle and London: University of Washington Press, 1966.

Gover, Charles E. *The Folk-Songs of Southern India*. Madras: The South India Saiva Siddhanta Works Publishing Society, 1959.

Gupta, Sankar Sen, ed. *The Patas and the Patuas of Bengal*. Calcutta: Indian Publications, 1973.

Joshi, O.P. *Painted Folklore and Folklore Painters of India*. Delhi: Concept Publishing Co, 1976.

Kurup, K.K.N. *The Cult of Teyyam and Hero Worship in Kerala*. Calcutta: Indian Publications, 1973.

Kothari Komal. "Epics of Rajasthan." *NCPA Quarterly Journal* (Bombay) XIII, No. 3 (September 1984).

Mahapatra, P.K. *The Folk Cults of Bengal*. Calcutta: Indian Publications, 1972.

Mukhopadhyay, Durgadas, ed. *Lesser Known Forms of Performing Arts in India*. New Delhi: Sterling Publishers Pvt. Ltd., 1978.

Thomas, P. *Hindu Religion, Customs and Manners*. Bombay: D.B. Taraporevala Sons & Co. Pvt. Ltd., 1956.

Vatsyayan, Kapila. *Traditions of Indian Folk Dance*. Delhi: Indian Book Company, 1976.

Vatuk, Ved Prakash. *Studies in Indian Folk Traditions*. New Delhi: Manohar, 1979.

Wade, Bonnie C., ed. *Performing Arts in India*. Berkeley: University of California, 1983.

Wilson, H.H. *et. al. The Theatre of the Hindus*. Calcutta: Sushil Gupta (India) Ltd., 1955.

The Ritual
Arts of India
Stella Kramrisch

Footnotes

1. Shilparatna of Shrī Kumāra, 46, 143-145, Trivandrum Sanskrit Series 75, 98, Trivandrum, 1922, 1929.

2. C.W. Crooke, *The Popular Religion and Folklore in Northern India*, vol. 2, London 1896, p. 191.

3. A. K. Coomaraswamy, *La Sculpture de Bharhut*, Paris, 1956, pl. XXXV, Fig. 102.

4. Joanna Gottfried Williams, *The Art of Gupta India*, Princeton, 1982, Figs. 254, 258; Louis Fréderic, *The Art of India*, New York, (no date) Fig. 79.

5. *The Arts of India*, ed. Basil Gray, Oxford, 1981, Fig. 11.

6. *Archaeological Survey of India, Annual Report*, 1930-1934, p. 99.

7. *The Great Bronze Age of China*, ed. Wen Fong, New York, 1980, p. 52.

8. *loc. cit.* Pls. 18, 20.

9. Keith Critchlow, *Islamic Patterns*, New York, 1976, p. 8.

10. The documentation by Jogendra Saksena, *The Art of Rajasthan*, Delhi, 1979, is the basis of the observations made in the present essay.

11. Red is the color of blood and life. It frightens away demons, (cf. note 2). A mud and brick dwelling of a neolithic settlement at Burzahom near Srinagar in Kashmir has its floor painted red, *Indian Archaeology, A Review*, New Delhi, 1961-62, p. 19.

12. The small surrounding devices are called chota mota māndnā.

13. Among the chota mota or surrounding devices of a māndnā, a few depict rather awkwardly an object such as a mango or a sword (Saksena, Pl. 41-43). Such depictions are not part of the traditional style of māndnā design. They are intrusions from the local popular art of the present or the recent past.

14. Laddu is the name of a round sweet. The names of the several motifs refer to various objects such as types of architecture—a town or well—and others such as a fan, flower, fruit, or a ritual object (hīr).

15. Archana Shastri, *Language of Symbols*, a project on South Indian Ritual Decorations of semi-permanent nature, submitted to All India Handicrafts Board, Dec. 1981, page preceding Fig. 25.

16. Tapan Mohan Chatterji, *Alpona*, Bombay, Orient Longman Ltd., 1948, p. 45.

17. *Ibid*, p. 8.

18. *Ibid*, p. 24.

19. Only about thirty million are counted today as tribal. Practically half of the tribal population of middle and south India does not declare itself as Hindu.

20. Illustrations and information from Verrier Elwin, *The Tribal Art of Middle India*, Oxford University Press, 1957.

21. Elwin, Figs. 214-216.

Index

(Numbers in italics indicate pages on which illustrations appear.)

Rāma, 52, 58, 142, 154, 188, 191, 192, 203, 205
Rāmāyana, 58, 129, 172, 188, 192, 201, 215, 224, 229
Rām Līlā, *154*, *172*, 197, 229, 236
Ramnagar, 229, 236
Rām, Tukā, 36
Rangolī, 60, 249
Rangpur, 260
Ratha Yātra, *173*
Rāvana, 129, *154*, 192; mask, *172*
Rawal, 262
Reverence for the sun, 106
Rig Veda, 31, 33, 188, 194, 261
Ritual art, 249-69; wall painting, *248*
Roof tiles (terra cotta), *124*, *125*
Rosewater sprinkler (brass), *80*
Royal procession, 67
Russell, R. V., 241

S

Sādhu, (Sādhū) *120*, 216, 230
Sadyojāta—Mother and Child, *105*
Saint (pīr), 173
Samskāra, 32, 136, 158, 212, 213, 216, 226, 249, 256. See also individual rites.
Sāng, 242
Sankarāchārya, 158
Sanskrit, 175, 198, 224; Sanskritic, 81
Santal, 258
Saora, 266, 268; Saora picture, *266*, *267*
Saperā, 79, 241
Sarasvatī (Saraswatī), 152
Sarkī band, 241
Sarpam pāttu, 234
Sathya, 249
Saurashtra, 249
Sāvitrī, 152
Schechner, Richard, 219, 221
Serving dish, Nagaland (bamboo), *137*
Shadipur, 167, 238, 240, 242, 243, 245
Shadipur mother, *108*
Shakti, 43
Shakuntalā, 202
Shaman, 228; shamanistic healer, 243
Sharma, B. G., 68
Shravana Belgola, *173*
Shashtī (terra cotta), *117*; 194, 253
Shashtī and Child (terra cotta), *104*
Shastri, Archana, 252

Shiau, *120*
Sindūr (vermillion), 60, 63, 76
Sindūr dān, 76
Shishu, 210
Shishya (learner), 158
Shītalā, 124
Shiva, *35*, 42, *44*, 45, 49, 58, *59*, 187, 191-92, 231, 263
Shivpur, 40
Shūdra (Sūdra), 238
Shrāddha (Shrādha), 27
Sickle, ritual, *38*
Sikh, 81, 82, 155, 170, 173; wedding, *74*
Sind, 258, 261
Singha (lion) (Sinha), *126*
Sītā, 52, 58, 129, 154, 191, 192
Sixty-four classical arts of ancient India, 60, 257
Snake, *45*, 253. See also Kundalinī.
Snake charmer, 228, *228*. See also Saperā, Jogī.
Snake dance, 79. See also Saperā.
Snake ritual, 234. See also Sarpam pāttu.
Sohar, 106, 209, 213.
Soma, Jivya, 52, 268
Soma (moon), 188-89, 190
Sonārākhnā, 249
"Song of the Way," 178
Song, birth, 106, 209, 213; cradle, 227; devotional, 139, 227, 228; marriage, 74, 79, 89; mehndī, 65; of the Way, 178; pīdo, 95; pregnancy, 98; propiatory, 124
Spirit Rider (Gothriz Purvez), 259-61, *261*
Storekeeper, Aurangabad, *164*
Story scroll, parh, *149*; patuā, 162. See also Parh.
Storysinger, 243
Storyteller, 198, 233, 241
Stupa, 259
Sufi, 236
Sun, 251. See also Sūrya.
Sūrdās, 205
Sūrya, 146, 188-89, 190-91
Sūryā, 188-89, 190-91
Swallowing, first (gutkī), 104

T

Tagore, Rabindranath, 178
Tamāshā, 236
Tamil lullaby, 115
Tamil Nadu, 38, 80, 98, 115, 234, 252

Tāntric ritual, 256
Teacher, 152, 158. See also Guru, Ustād.
Telengana, 252
Temple , Portable (wood), *155*
Teyyam, 233
Thirumalai Nāyaka, King, 86
Thoibi, 225
Thorī, 243
Thread, sacred, *159*, 186, 223, 249
Tiger (wood), *129*
Tīkā, 71
Tobacco container, *76*
Tobacco pipe, *53*
Toda, 259
Tonsure (mundan), 213
Toran, 71, *89*
Toy maker, 132
Toys, 132; horse-drawn cart, *127*; iron monkeys, *128*; kneeling elephant, *129*; lion, *126*; mother-and-child dolls, *106*, *107*; mother-and-daughter rag dolls, *128*
Toy seller, Madras, *128*
Tribes and Castes of the Central Provinces of India, The, Russell, 241
Trichur, 136
Trija janma, 27
Tukā Rām, see Rām, Tukā
Tulsīdās, 205, 206
Turtle, 43, *63*
Twice-born, 136, 158, 162, 186. See also Dvija.

U

Udal, 229-30
Umā, *45*
Upanayana ceremony (Upanayanam), 158, 187, 216, 223
Urs, 236
Ustād (teacher), 155, 162
Uttanapad, 32
Uttar Pradesh, 230, 242, 249

V

Vaishya, 238
Vallabhacharya, 142
Vālmīki, 229
Varanasi (Benares), 46, 146; boys learn by helping at, *157*
Vāsant (spring festival), 129
Vāsudeva, King, 194

Vedic, Aryan society, 223; funeral ceremony, 196; marriage hymn, 191; period, 186; thought, 43
Vegetable cutter (iron), *72*
Veil, pīdo, *93*, *95*
Vermillion (sindūr), 60, 63, 76, 89, 172, 252-53
Vidyārambha, 216
Village bards, *229*
Villupāttu, 234
Vindhya range, 260
Vīra, *44*
Vishnu, 43, 188, 194
Vishvanātha, 148
Vishvāvasu, 189-90
Votive plaques (silver), *125*
Vow (vrata), 249, 253
Vraja, 54
Vrata, 249, 253

W

Waha, 262
Walker for child, *143*
Warli, 52, 266, 268; paintings, *52*, *269*
Water pot/jar, 38, *39*, *40*, 77, *138*, *139*. See also Gagarā, Lotā.
"Way of Grace," 142
Weaving, 163
Wedding, 57-83, *81*, 228, 243; Hindu, *82*; Sikh, *74*; tribal, Arunachal Pradesh, *75*
Wedding blouse (choli), *75*
Wedding feast, 79
Wedding motifs, 58
Wedding procession, 67-71; song, 68
Wedding response, 74
Womb, 46. See also Yoni.
Worshipping (pūjā), 173
Window shutter (painted wood), *119*
Women churning, *47*; Leather puppet, *47*

Y

Yakshagāna, 233
Yantra, 256
Yashodā, 128, 139, 193, 205
Yashodā and Krishna (wood), *104*
Yoga, 32
Yoni, 43, 44

Z

Zarathustra (Zoroaster), 159
Zoroastrian, 81

Picture Credits

Legend

B bottom   R right
C center   T top
L left

Cover Daphne Shuttleworth
Back Cover Tony Heiderer

Front Matter p. 1-2 Chip Clark/
Smithsonian Institution (SI); 4-5
Tony Heiderer; 7 Roland &
Sabrina Michaud; 8 Kim Nielsen;
10 S. Paul; 14 S. Paul; 16
Jyoti Rath; 17 Roland & Sabrina
Michaud; 18 Yog Joy; 19 Jyoti
Rath; 24 Lance Dane; 25 Mark
Edwards; 26 Chip Clark/SI; 27 ©
Yves Véquaud. From: *The Women
Painters of Mithila* by Yves
Véquaud. © 1976 Les Presses de la
Connaissance, Paris. © 1977
Thames and Hudson Ltd.,
London; 29 Dilip Sinha; 32 Jyoti
Rath.

I. Fertility pp. 35 Elizabeth S.
Miles/MFM; 36-37 S. Paul; 38
Chip Clark/SI; 39 George Rogers/
Magnum; 40 Tejbir Singh; 41 Jyoti
Rath; 42T Roland & Sabrina
Michaud; B Daphne Shuttleworth;
43 Jyoti Rath; 44T Roland &
Sabrina Michaud; B Lance Dane;
45 Jyoti Rath; 46T J.H.C. Wilson/
Robert Harding Picture Library; B
Avinash Pasricha; 47T Francis
Wacziarg & Aman Nath; B Jyoti
Rath; 48T Chip Clark/SI; B Dilip
Sinha; 49T Jyoti Rath; B Lance
Dane.

II. Courtship and Betrothal pp. 51
Dilip Sinha; 52 Lance Dane; 53T
Chip Clark; L&R Jyoti Rath; 54-55
Jyoti Rath.

III. Preparation for the Wedding
pp. 56 Chip Clark/SI; 57 Aman
Nath; 58 Dilip Sinha; 59 © Yves
Véquaud. From: *The Women
Painters of Mithila* by Yves
Véquaud. © 1976 Les Presses de la
Connaissance, Paris. © 1977
Thames and Hudson Ltd.,
London. 60 Christopher Sholes; 61
Dilip Sinha; 62-63 Jyoti Rath; 64
Marilyn Silverstone/Magnum; 65T
Elizabeth S. Miles/MFM; B Chip
Clark/SI.

IV. The Wedding Procession pp. 67
Lance Dane; 68 Tejbir Singh; 69
Frances C. Rowsell; 70 Dilip Sinha;
71 Tony Heiderer.

V. The Wedding pp. 72-73 Jyoti
Rath; 74 Marilyn Silverstone/
Magnum; 75T T.S. Satyan; B Jyoti
Rath; 76-77, 78T Chip Clark/SI; B

Ashok Khanna; 79 Roland &
Sabrina Michaud; 80 Chip Clark/
SI; 81 Bernard Pierre Wolff/
Magnum; 82T Marilyn Silverstone/
Magnum; B Jyoti Rath; 83T & BL
Tejbir Singh; R Chip Clark/SI.

VI. The Wedding Night pp. 84-85
Tony Heiderer; 87-90 Jyoti Rath;
91 Roland & Sabrina Michaud.

VII. Conception pp. 93 Lance
Dane; 94 Jyoti Rath; 95 Rajeev
Sethi.

VIII. Pregnancy pp. 97 Roland &
Sabrina Michaud; 98-99 Chip
Clark/SI.

IX. Birth pp. 101-104 Jyoti Rath;
105 Lance Dane; 106 Chip Clark/
SI; 107T T.S. Nagarajan; B Chip
Clark/SI.

X. Welcoming the Child pp. 108
Daphne Shuttleworth; 109 Lance
Dane; 110T Chip Clark/SI; B
Elizabeth S. Miles/MFM; 111 S.
Paul; 112-113L&R Chip Clark/SI;
B Lance Dane; 114T Tony
Heiderer; B S. Paul; 115T
Christopher Sholes; B Tony
Heiderer.

XI. Safeguarding the Child pp. 116-
117 Chip Clark/SI; 118 Christopher
Sholes; 119 Chip Clark/SI; 120T
Stephen Huyler; B Jyoti Rath; 121
Dilip Sinha; 122-123 Jyoti Rath;
124T Christopher Sholes; B Jyoti
Rath; 125T&B Chip Clark/SI; R
Jyoti Rath.

XII. The Promised World pp. 126-
127 Jyoti Rath; 128T Antonio
Martinelli/Roberto Meazza; B Yog
Joy; L Jyoti Rath; 129 Chip Clark/
SI; 130 Dilip Sinha; T Tejbir
Singh; B Chip Clark; 131 Tony
Heiderer; 132 Jyoti Rath; 133L
T.S. Satyan; R Jyoti Rath.

XIII. First Feeding pp. 135-136
Chip Clark/SI; 137T Pepita Noble;
L Marilyn Silverstone/Magnum; R
Chip Clark/SI; 138 Chip Clark/SI;
139 Jyoti Rath.

XIV. The First Step pp. 141 Chip
Clark/SI; 143 Michael Freeman.

XV. Initiation into Learning pp. 145
Adam Woolfitt/Susan Griggs
Agency; 146 Dilip Sinha; 147
Stella Snead; 148 S.

Anandalakshmy; 149T Dilip Sinha;
B Daphne Shuttleworth; 150L
Jyoti Rath; 150R-151 Mary Ellen
Mark/Archive Pictures Inc.; 152T
Dilip Sinha; B Tony Heiderer;
153T Lance Dane; B Raghubir
Singh; R Jyoti Rath; 154T Chip
Clark/SI; B Sondeep Shankar;
155T Mary Ellen Mark/Archive
Pictures Inc.; L Dilip Sinha; R
Elizabeth S. Miles, MFM.

XVI. Learning To Be and To Do
pp. 156 Mary Ellen Mark/Archive
Pictures Inc.; 157 Paul L.
Kuepferle; 158 Antonio Martinelli/
Roberto Meazza; 159 Raghubir
Singh; 160 Antonio Martinelli/
Roberto Meazza; 161 Chip Clark/
SI; 162 Marc Riboud/Magnum;
163 Dilip Sinha; 164-165 Bernard
Pierre Wolfe/Magnum; 166 Dilip
Sinha; 167 Tony Heiderer.

XVII. Fairs and Festivals pp. 168-
169 Antonio Martinelli/Roberto
Meazza; 170T Jyoti Rath; B
Jehangir Gazdar/Woodfin Camp &
Assoc.; 171T Tony Heiderer; L
Jehangir Gazdar/Woodfin Camp &
Assoc.; R Roland & Sabrina
Michaud; 172T R. Bedi; B Chip
Clark/SI; 173 Jehangir Gazdar/
Woodfin Camp & Assoc.; 174-
175T Tony Heiderer; B Jyoti Rath;
176T Air India Library; B Daphne
Shuttleworth; 177 Jehangir Gazdar/
Woodfin Camp & Assoc.

Moving Out pp. 178 Roland &
Sabrina Michaud; 179 Frances C.
Rowsell; 180-183 Jehangir Gazdar/
Woodfin Camp & Assoc.

*The Role of Myth in the Indian Life
Cycle* pp. 184 Freer Gallery of Art/
SI; 186 J.H.C. Wilson/Robert
Harding Picture Library;
188 Lance Dane; 191 Jyoti
Rath; 192 Jehangir Gazdar/
Woodfin Camp & Assoc. 193T
Chip Clark/SI; B Roland & Sabrina
Michaud; 195L Roland & Sabrina
Michaud; R Chip Clark/SI; 196
Roland & Sabrina Michaud; 197
Dilip Sinha; 198 From: *Amar
Chitra Katha, Tales of Durgā* ©
India Book House Education
Trust, Bombay; 199 Dilip Sinha.

The Child in India pp. 200 Stella
Snead; 202L Christopher Sholes; R
Daphne Shuttleworth; 206 Jyoti
Rath; 208 B.S. Dhillon; 210 Dilip
Sinha; 212 Christopher Sholes; 213

Antonio Martinelli/Roberto
Meazza; 215 Tony Heiderer; 217
Dilip Sinha.

Performance, Music, and the Child
pp. 218 Dilip Sinha; 220 R. Bedi;
221 Ian Berry/Magnum; 222T
Tejbir Singh; B Jyoti Rath; 224
Nazir A. Jairazbhoy; 225 Jehangir
Gazdar/Woodfin Camp & Assoc.;
226-229L Roland & Sabrina
Michaud; R Tony Heiderer; 230
Jehangir Gazdar/Susan Griggs
Agency; 232 Frances C. Rowsell;
233 Chip Clark; 234 Jyoti Rath;
235 Avinash Pasricha; 237 Michael
Freeman; 239 Nazir A. Jairazbhoy;
240 Dilip Sinha; 242 Nazir A.
Jairazbhoy; 245 Antonio Martinelli/
Roberto Meazza.

The Ritual Arts of India pp. **68**
Yves Véquaud; 248 Stella Snead;
249-251T Reproduced from: *Art of
Rajasthan* (plates 43, 42, 64, 65, &
27) by Jogendra Saksena.
Published by Swadesh Prasad
Singhal for Sundeep Prakashan,
Delhi; 251B Reproduced from:
Pahari Folk Art (Fig. 20) by O.C.
Handa. Published by D.B.
Taraporevala Sons & Co. Pvt.
Ltd.; 252T Collection Pupul
Jayakar. Photography by Jyoti
Rath; 252B-253T,B Reproduced
from: *Language of Symbols* (Figs.
265, 40, & 179) by Archana
Shastri. All India Handicrafts
Board, Crafts Council, Madras;
254T Reproduced from: *Alpona*
(no. 19) by Mohan Chatterji.
Published by Orient Longmans
Ltd., Bombay; B From the
catalogue *Unknown India: Ritual
Art in Tribe and Village* (plate
XLII) © Philadelphia Museum of
Art, 1968. Lent anonymously; 257
Jyoti Rath; 261 From the catalogue
*Unknown India: Ritual Art in Tribe
and Village* (plate XIV) ©
Philadelphia Museum of Art, 1968.
Lent anonymously; 263 © Harry
Holtzman. From the catalogue
*Unknown India: Ritual Art in Tribe
and Village* © Philadelphia
Museum of Art, 1968. 266-267
Reproduced from: *The Tribal Art
of Middle India* (Figs. 214 & 222)
by Verrier Elwin. Published by
Geoffrey Cumberlege, Oxford
University Press. 269 Reproduced
from the magazine *Marg* Vol.
XXXIV, No. 4, Bombay.

Artisans and Performers for Aditi—A Celebration of Life

Courtship and Betrothal
Jivya Soma, wall painter, Maharashtra

Preparation for the Wedding
Ganga Devi, painter, Bihar

The Wedding Procession
Mithu Ram, horse dancer, Haryana
Ramesh Tandon, musician and dancer, Rajasthan

The Wedding
Chandrakala Devi, sculptor, Bihar
Mahadev Nath, musician, Rajasthan
Sarvan Nath, musician, Rajasthan
Gulabi Nath, dancer, Rajasthan
Rajki Nath, dancer, Rajasthan

Conception
Amina Bai Ismail Khatri, veil maker, Gujarat

Pregnancy
Saraswathy Basavaraju, glass painter, Karnataka
R. Eswarlal, glass painter, Tamil Nadu

Welcoming the Child
Nizamuddin Langa, musician and singer, Rajasthan
Rehmat Khan Langa, musician and singer, Rajasthan
Bundu Khan, musician and singer, Rajasthan
Bundu Kohinur Khan, musician and singer, Rajasthan

Safeguarding the Child
M. Palaniappan, potter, Tamil Nadu
Jhithru Ram Kumhar, potter, Madhya Pradesh

The Promised World
Kumudini Devi, grass weaver, Bihar
Mohammad Chand Pasha, magician, Andhra Pradesh
Mohammad Yusef, magician, Andhra Pradesh
Sagar Bhatt, puppeteer, Rajasthan
Puran Bhatt, puppeteer, puppet maker and musician, Rajasthan
Bhagwan Dass Bhatt, musician and singer, Rajasthan

Initiation into Learning
Balraj Shetty, juggler, Andhra Pradesh
Ram Karan, balladeer, Rajasthan
Gotli Devi, story scroll singer, Rajasthan
Shish Ram, dancer, Rajasthan
Kailash, dancer, Rajasthan

Learning To Be and To Do
Bhaskar Mahapatra, painter, Orissa
Subir Pal, toy maker, West Bengal
Banku Patua, scroll artist and singer, West Bengal
Gurupada Chitrakar, scroll artist and singer, West Bengal

Fairs and Festivals
Chiranji Bahurupiya, impersonator, Rajasthan
Krishan, impersonator, Haryana
Sona Bai, acrobat, Maharashtra
Dev Chand, acrobat, Maharashtra
Krishna Bai, acrobat, Rajasthan
Dharam Pal, acrobat, Uttar Pradesh

Narpat Singh Rathore, manager, Rajasthan